If It's Broken, You Can Fix It

If It's Broken, You Can Fix It

Overcoming Dysfunction in the Workplace

Tom E. Jones

WORxPublishing

Fresno

This book is available at a special
discount when ordered in bulk quantities.
For information, contact WORx Publishing.
5555 N. West Ave. #133
Fresno CA 93711

This publication is designed to provide accurate and authoritative information in regard to the subject matter covered. It is sold with the understanding that the publisher is not engaged in rendering legal, accounting, or other professional service. If legal advice or other expert assistance is required, the services of a competent professional person should be sought.

Library of Congress Cataloging-in-Publication Data

Jones, Tom E.
If it's broken, you can fix it : overcoming dysfunction in the workplace / Tom E. Jones.
p. cm.
Includes bibliographical references and index.
ISBN 0-9649080-2-6 (previously ISBN 0-8144-0460-X)
1. Management. 2. Communication in management.
3. Organizational effectiveness. I. Title.
HD31.J6343 1998
658.4′063—dc21 *98–35079*
CIP

Printed in the United States of America.

Printing number

10 9 8 7 6 5 4 3 2 1

To

Bob Tannenbaum

for those insightful visits to the rock,
for your strong spirit and generous nature,
for those caring nudges and gentle persuasions,
for your warm and welcome friendship.

Contents

List of Figures

Foreword

"Uncovering dysfunction in the workplace is like locating termites in your house," says author Tom Jones. "You may suspect they're there because you've seen the signs, but you don't know where they are or how to get at them." *If It's Broken, You Can Fix It* introduces techniques for exposing—and managing—dysfunctional behaviors, and shows you how to build and foster a successful team despite a dysfunctional environment. As the author explains, "The premise of this book is that mainstream management methods don't work in a dysfunctional workplace. In this setting, you will need a different set of tools."

This book provides managers (not just human resources professionals) with insights into human behavior, enabling human beings and organizations to better facilitate change. Change is always resisted, and organizational change has an 85 percent mortality rate. The single greatest source of resistant to change in organizations? Dysfunctional people. *If It's Broken, You Can Fix It* brings the negative behavior of the dysfunctional employee, with its enormous cost to organizations, out of the closet. For the first time, it fully exposes the largely unexplored role that dysfunction plays in halting organizational change.

Implementing the tools and techniques presented in this book will help managers contribute to productivity and organizational success by improving the humanness of their organizations. Readers will find wide-ranging insights that will enable them to recognize the subtle behavior patterns that have stifled organizations for years. Fortunately, Tom Jones does not stop at recognition of these dysfunctional behaviors—he also provides recipes that creative chefs can use to actually stop the dysfunction.

The book is filled with pragmatic, sequential tips for solving the problem of dysfunction in the workplace. It is a gold mine of informational nuggets. Some of the nuggets are "best of breed" from recent management literature; some derive from Tom Jones's thirty years of experience as a successful organizational development consultant; and some have been culled directly from organizations, both public and private, that have broken new ground in developing tools and strategies to ameliorate dysfunctional behavior. *If It's Broken, You Can Fix It* builds upon the work of others and fully integrates the tips and techniques of other professionals who have contributed to the practice of more effective management.

Good managers are made, not born. Thus it is incumbent on all of us to increase our knowledge base and skills. This book highlights the importance of a variety of leadership skills, including setting direction, maintaining a sense of fun, and creating an environment in which real teams can be built. It specifically highlights the leadership skill of coaching. Successful managers have long recognized, but often forget, that different people learn in different ways, and that effective coaches work on different skills (or the lack thereof) with each member of the team.

This book offers a lot of bang for the buck. It's also very user-friendly. Unlike many management books, which read like dusty college texts, this one is written in the first person. If you've ever had a chance to hear Tom Jones speak in person, you will recognize his voice in these pages. His personal narratives convey his insights most effectively.

—Ted Gaebler, President,
The Gaebler Group, Inc.,
and co-author of *Reinventing Government*

Preface

"Making your way in the world today takes everything you've got." This catchy tune from the TV show *Cheers* captures the essence of a worrisome issue. Today's managers *are* giving it everything they've got, but it never seems to be enough.

Contemporary managers face the external pressures of new technologies, converging markets, evolving consumers, and workforces that are undergoing transformation. It's no wonder that so many of them are unsure how to prepare for the challenge of change. One participant at a recent conference on total quality management expressed his frustration very clearly. "This quality stuff sounds great," he said, "but it won't work in my company. In fact, we're so messed up, *nothing* I do works anymore."

This simple truth unleashed a flood of affirmations from the other managers in the audience, and I spent the rest of the session helping them process their pent-up frustrations. Many incidents similar to this have convinced me that today's managers are stymied by their inability to determine the course of their future.

As a recent Associated Press headline declared, "Hierarchy is out and small business units, empowered workers, and customer-driven processes are in." Organizations are getting lean and mean—they are downsizing by paring back both the layers and the ranks of managers. This trend originated in the 1980s and has been perpetuated by a growing number of high-profile author/consultants who focus on management as the problem. Consider the following quotes from popular management gurus of that era:

"Management doesn't make the company, it's the guy on the loading dock who decides not to drop the box."

—Tom Peters, *In Search of Excellence,* 1982

"The sharp distinction between 'management' and 'workers' possible in the old organizational era is no longer as clear in the new one."

—Rosabeth Moss Kanter, *The Change Masters,* 1983

"So much of what we call management consists of making it difficult for people to work."

—Peter F. Drucker, *The Frontiers of Management,* 1986

"The ability to manage well doesn't make much difference if you're not even in the 'right jungle.' "

—Stephen R. Covey,
The 7 Habits of Highly Effective People, 1989

Pithy phrases like those set the stage for a proliferation of seminars, workshops, and training programs, each touted as the pathway to managerial competence. Rather than raising awareness, these management-targeted skill-building programs instead created doubt and turned many guilt-laden managers into seminar junkies in search of a quick fix.

Our organizations expect managers to plan, organize, direct, and control every move. Should performance and productivity fall off, management shoulders the blame. A few managers get fired, a pointed reminder of what happens to those who fail. Then a consultant is brought in to conduct an organizationwide fact-finding survey. The goal is simple: Identify the problem(s) and get the organization back on track. Invariably, the consultant determines that management needs more training. Those managers who wish to keep their jobs dutifully attend the latest "buzzword" program. Yet once the dust settles—despite all the time, talent, and treasure invested—nothing improves. Production usually continues to decline, and the situation deteriorates. Why? Because the organization never addressed the root of the problem.

The underlying problem is managerial, but the solution lies outside the scope of mainstream methods. Mainstream authors write as though our organizations and the people in them were functional. The tools, techniques, and methods promoted by mainstream training programs are primarily designed for use in *functional* environments. But while experts in mainstream theories are promoting teamwork and participation, more and more managers are finding themselves in situations in which those mainstream methods simply don't work.

If you listen to managers describe these situations, you find a definite pattern emerging: Their employees are displaying what behavioral science would call *dysfunctional behavior.* Dysfunctional behavior is characterized by unstable relationships, harmful habits, poor organization, lack of confidence, and the inability to make good choices. While such behavior is not new to the workplace, it is becoming more commonplace and thus increasingly difficult to handle.

Psychotherapists, family counselors, and social workers have all voiced concern about this phenomenon, and are acutely aware of the negative changes in the social-behavioral patterns of the families and individuals who are now turning to them for help. Current reports on people seeking counseling show that upwards of 90 percent spent all or some of their formative years in a dysfunctional family, social, or institutional environment. Many have turned to counseling out of frustration, hampered by limited social skills, poor problem-solving and decision-making capabilities, and an inability to succeed on their own initiative. These individuals commonly express potent feelings of fear, guilt, and anger as they dig into the root causes of their problems.

These individuals don't leave their societal dysfunctions at home when they come to work. They share them with the organization. On the job, they have difficulty coping with ambiguity and adjusting to change. Their lack of trust impairs their ability to deal openly and honestly with coworkers. Dysfunctional employees rely heavily on clearly structured relationships for approval and acceptance. They want to know who's responsible for what. They resist participating in teams, tend to avoid responsibility, and prefer to work alone.

You need look no further than the rapid growth of employer-sponsored behavioral counseling and substance abuse programs to see that more and more people in today's workforce are struggling with dysfunctional behaviors. These people are having a negative impact on our organizations by creating corresponding dysfunction in the workplace. They are legion—and their numbers are growing.

The level of dysfunction within our organizations has reached the point where it needs our immediate attention. As more and more dysfunctional behaviors are brought into the workplace, the makeup of our organizations will continue to change. So must our management strategies.

We need to adopt a new perspective in order to keep our organizations, and the people they employ, from becoming more dysfunctional. The perspective offered in this book stems from thirty years of working, consulting, and training in dysfunctional settings. The book provides a collection of simple ideas woven together through practice and experimentation. Not all of these ideas work all of the time, but all of them have worked at one time or another in a variety of difficult situations.

I hope they work for you.

—Tom E. Jones

Acknowledgments

One does not write a book in a vacuum. Without the efforts of many dedicated people, this book would still be a collection of notes, commentaries, and articles. First, I wish to acknowledge those established management theorists and mainstream authors who gave me something to push against. Their groundbreaking efforts and professional leadership raised the corporate consciousness and helped create the audience for this book.

Thanks to the many employees within the client organizations who not only allowed me to work with them, but tolerated—and in some cases encouraged—my experimentation with new models, methods, and concepts. These courageous, adventuresome people willingly provided a laboratory for my consulting practice. I am honored to have had the privilege of working with all of them.

Many friends and colleagues have given freely and frequently of their time, talents, and treasures in the advancement of this venture. I greatly appreciate the many contributions of Alan Sevener, Ken Pascal, Nancy Calhoun, Julie Wilson, Keith Pipes, and Thom Bardwell.

My thanks to the many reviewers of the manuscript whose valued comments and criticisms helped to shape a better book: Pat Hosegood Martin, Kerry Miller, Peggy Anderson, Pauline Jones, John Chapleau, Alison Delaney, Donna Hall, and Wink Chase.

I was constantly awed by the technical contributions of these highly talented professionals, whose skills I could not have done without: Charles Shields, Toby Eskola, Michael Delaney, Ivonne Der Torosian, and Niels Buessem.

A very special thanks to my gifted friend Marsha Anderson, whose quick wit, professional advice, and gentle persuasions made writing this book a joyful experience.

Finally, I acknowledge my wife, Pauline. I deeply appreciate all the love and support you provided along the way. I apologize for the many hours of mental absence and promise to make them up to you, soon.

1

Assessing Dysfunction

Webster's New World Dictionary defines *dysfunction* as "abnormal, impaired, or incomplete functioning." Most of us think of dysfunction as a family issue. Because of its personal nature, dysfunctional behavior in the workplace is not widely discussed. However, not talking about it doesn't mean it isn't present.

Dysfunction in the workplace has probably been there for quite a while. If you don't hear much about it where you work, that may simply mean that your organization hasn't put it on the table as a management issue. Managers should not only be talking about organizational dysfunction, but also be finding ways to overcome it before *their* ability to function is impaired.

Much like a family, an organization becomes dysfunctional when its members lack the confidence, ability, or desire to pull together. When employees don't get along at work, their individual job performances suffer and their mutual efforts level off or decline. Given that the function of an organization or family is to create a place where individuals achieve collectively what they cannot do alone, it makes sense to say that when an organization or family can no longer do this, it has become dysfunctional.

Like a contagious disease, dysfunctional attitudes and behaviors can spread from person to person and from unit to unit. If the condition is left undiagnosed, it is possible for an entire organization to become dysfunctional and still not know it is "sick."

In order to overcome whatever dysfunction may exist in your workplace, you must first learn to recognize dysfunctional behaviors. It is difficult to change these behaviors unless you understand what they are and how they can negatively affect you.

Dysfunctional Behaviors

In their highly informative book *The Addictive Organization,* psychologists Anne Wilson Schaef and Diane Fassel identify behaviors that contribute to dysfunction in addictive organizations.* After spending years consulting with a variety of dysfunctional organizations, I have added several items to their original set, identifying dysfunctional behaviors that may be present in *any* organization. The resulting list of twenty specific behaviors, in checklist format, is shown in Figure 1-1. The checklist is followed by a description of each behavior. Are any of the behaviors on this list common in your organization? Check them off. Then note the number of checkmarks you have made. Use the results to assess the current level of dysfunction in your organization or work unit.

The greater the number of checks, the greater the level of dysfunction. Keep the results of this checklist handy. As you weave your way through the book, use the specific items you've checked to develop an action plan. If you really feel brave, give a copy of the checklist to everyone on your team to complete. Then bring your team members together to share the results. The comparison between your list and their lists would make an interesting and worthwhile discussion topic for your next meeting.

*Anne Wilson Schaef and Diane Fassel, *The Addictive Organization* (New York: Harper & Row, 1988). Copyright © 1988 by Anne Wilson Schaef and Diane Fassel. Reprinted by permission of HarperCollins Publishers, Inc.

Figure 1-1. Dysfunctional behaviors checklist.

- ❑ Communication is indirect.
- ❑ Conflicts are not stated openly.
- ❑ Secrets are used to build alliances.
- ❑ Gossip is used to excite and titillate.
- ❑ Corporate memory is lost or forgotten.
- ❑ Requests for policy clarification are ignored.
- ❑ The open expression of true feelings is absent.
- ❑ The search for the cause of a problem is personalized.
- ❑ People look for direction on how to act and react.
- ❑ Friendship between professional colleagues is lacking.
- ❑ Complex procedures are initiated by memorandum.
- ❑ Meetings have long agendas and end up going in circles.
- ❑ Inconsistent application of procedures is not challenged.
- ❑ Mundane announcements are given too much time at meetings.
- ❑ Promises of better times ahead seduce people into a status quo.
- ❑ Dualistic (us versus them) thinking creates conflict and sets up sides.
- ❑ Perfectionism creates an atmosphere of intolerance for mistakes.
- ❑ Judgments are made about people being "good" or "bad."
- ❑ Isolation keeps management from seeing what is happening.
- ❑ Management isolation is used as the basis of decision making by cliques.

Total items checked: __________

The greater the number of checks, the greater the level of dysfunction. Keep the results of the checklist handy. As you proceed, use the specific items you've checked to develop an action plan.

❑ Communication is indirect.

People don't talk to one another face-to-face. Instead, they find an alternative method of conveying information—especially if the message is bad news, if it is likely to create hard feelings, or if it may bring up an uncomfortable issue. Indirect communication is common between individuals or groups who have a long-standing feud or just don't get along. A third party may be asked to deliver the message but instructed not to reveal the sender's identity.

❑ Conflicts are not stated openly.

Differences between coworkers remain hidden from the collective view. People keep track of things that upset others and make sure they do not bring these things up during meetings. The deeper, more potent issues are put on the "no-no" list and never mentioned in front of "them." Spirited debates center on nonthreatening issues such as where to hold the Christmas party; which office supply vendor to use; or who is authorized to park in the reserved spaces.

❑ Secrets are used to build alliances.

Individuals with confidential or privileged information disclose it to a chosen few. Sensitive information is passed with this caveat attached: *Promise you won't tell anyone. If it gets out that I told you, I'm in big trouble.* In turn, these confidants are expected to share any private tidbits that come their way. Thus, an alliance is formed of insiders who feel involved and included. Meanwhile, those outside the alliance feel alienated and excluded.

❑ Gossip is used to excite and titillate.

Everyone loves a juicy piece of gossip. Even if people don't want to believe it, they still want to hear it. The rumor mill usually carries harmless or amusing commentary. Unfortunately, some folks get a kick out of passing on unfounded or false stories just to get attention. The mean-spirited passing of false accusations and malicious hearsay harms innocent people. Reputations are damaged, credibility is lost, and employee morale suffers.

- ❑ Corporate memory is lost or forgotten.

  Records of previous agreements can't be found. Projects get started, then are stopped suddenly without explanation. Problems that were thought to have been solved resurface. Work is often duplicated for no apparent reason while similar tasks are forgotten or ignored. Quick fixes replace carefully thought-out solutions, and past mistakes are repeated. The primary mission is lost in a sea of special programs and pet projects.

- ❑ Requests for policy clarification are ignored.

  Those who raise policy questions in an open forum are frequently told, "I'll get back to you on that," or "Let me run that one by personnel," or "Stop by my office later and we'll talk about it." When the requesters do stop by, they're provided with justification rather than clarification. Written requests for policy guidance are never answered. Direct questions about policy implementation are met with hostility or defensiveness, but no answer.

- ❑ The open expression of true feelings is absent.

  People are uncomfortable about expressing how they *really* feel. If people know that their feelings will not be respected, they keep them hidden. Even when they strongly oppose the prevailing viewpoint, folks nod and give their OK. A show of feelings is avoided for fear of getting hurt. Those who do let their feelings out are labeled as *touchy-feely* and told to get a grip on reality. Employees rarely take time off and seldom go on vacation.

- ❑ The search for the cause of a problem is personalized.

  The key concern is who did it rather than what went wrong. Anyone with information keeps quiet until the search is over. People spend more time covering their tracks than looking for answers. The culprits are mentioned by name and held up as examples of what not to do. Personal responsibility and blame are considered one and the same. Volunteering information can be a career-ending experience, should the project go wrong.

- ❑ People look for direction on how to act and react.

  People wait to be told what to do because going ahead on their own is too risky. They've learned that even when they're told, *it's up to you*—it isn't. Folks decode body language and "read between the lines," looking for hidden agendas. Trial balloons are floated up the chain of command to test reactions and make sure upstairs is okay with it. Projects are piloted repeatedly to work out all the bugs before the final launch.

- ❑ Friendship between professional colleagues is lacking.

  Folks who work together don't seem to know much about one another. Opportunities for social interaction are rare and not well attended. People are seldom asked and rarely volunteer what's going on in their lives outside the workplace. Misunderstandings, mistrust, and miscommunication are taken for granted. Occasions for celebration like birthdays, anniversaries, awards, and promotions come and go with little fanfare.

- ❑ Complex procedures are initiated by memorandum.

  Major projects such as computer conversions, telephone installations, and office relocation are suddenly jump-started by a vaguely worded, half-page memo. Detailed guidelines are hard to find. Planning session schedules are rarely followed. When challenged to provide detailed guidelines, project directors apologize for the lack of specifics and promise to provide the relevant information as it becomes available.

- ❑ Meetings have long agendas and end up going in circles.

  New business is added after the agenda is published. Old business is revisited by those who aren't satisfied with or didn't understand the previous decision. Personal agendas are injected by the use of phrases like "This will only take a minute," "I hope no one has a problem with this," "There's just one thing that concerns me," or "I'm not sure I agree, totally." Meetings sometimes run so long that people will agree to anything just to get out of there.

- ❑ Inconsistent application of procedures is not challenged.

  Chaos and confusion typically follow the introduction of a new procedure. Directives are followed by some people but not by others, resulting in two different outcomes. No one points out the inconsistency or seeks clarification. When policies seem unfair or discriminatory, no one says anything. People work outside their job descriptions without complaint. When procedural changes are introduced at meetings, folks sit quietly without comment.

- ❑ Mundane announcements are given too much time at meetings.

  An analysis of the van pool ridership for the past three years tops the agenda. The instructions for completing a survey of photocopy needs are covered in detail. The catering contractor presents a categorized list of food service complaints together with the plan for corrective actions. A discussion of the facilities maintenance schedule and equipment replacement projections, tabled at the last session, will continue if time allows.

- ❑ Promises of better times ahead seduce people into a status quo.

  An unexpected rash of resignations is shrugged off as a knee-jerk reaction to a temporary downturn. Motivational speeches and rah-rah sessions increase for no apparent reason. Higher profit and sales forecasts are announced with great fanfare. The long-term growth projections are unrealistic, but most people accept the numbers. Folks pitch in, pull together, and give 110 percent, although their reasons for doing so aren't clear.

- ❑ Dualistic (us versus them) thinking creates conflict and sets up sides.

  When opposing viewpoints surface, people are forced to take a stand. Alternative options or compromise solutions are seldom explored. The challenge to be right stimulates opposing parties. People choose their side carefully because being on the losing end can have negative consequences. Group leaders use veiled threats to ensure allegiance; "Don't forget who's boss" and "It's my way or the highway" are two examples.

- ❑ Perfectionism creates an atmosphere of intolerance for mistakes.

  Micromanagers control every outcome. No matter how hard people work or how good they get, they're expected to do better. Criticism prevails; praise and recognition are nonexistent. Simple mistakes and innocent oversights are blown out of proportion. Employees are disciplined or demoted for minor infractions. Those who complete assignments ahead of schedule are given more work to do. Enough is never enough.

- ❑ Judgments are made about people being "good" or "bad."

  People are told, "That's a bad idea. It's a good thing you checked with me first." Promotions are based on how well people "fit." Personality is a critical factor in determining who gets along with whom. Employees who don't fit in are labeled as "bad" and are rarely given a second chance. A "good" employee is one who gets along well with coworkers and doesn't upset the boss. Job performance doesn't seem to matter.

- ❑ Isolation keeps management from seeing what is happening.

  Employees feel that management is out of touch and has no idea of what's going on. Long-standing personnel problems never get resolved. Complaints and concerns fall on deaf ears. Managers are too often out of town, away at a conference, or in a meeting. Electronic messaging and telephone technologies buffer management from the world outside. Managers have no idea what's important to the people who work for them.

- ❑ Management isolation is used as the basis of decision making by cliques.

  Like-minded people form small groups and set their own agendas. Groups compete for scarce resources and purposely withhold information from one another. Folks who show initiative are thought to have management's blessing. Group leaders with connections seem to get whatever equipment and personnel they need. Those outside the loop are still waiting for approval. Folks assume that if managers know, they must not care.

The items cited in Figure 1-1 and the expanded descriptions that you've just read are not meant to be all-inclusive. They are offered as an introduction to the types of dysfunctional behaviors that may be present in your organization. As you strive to uncover whatever dysfunction might exist in your workplace, you may discover some additional behaviors that are not listed here. If so, add them to the pile and work them into your action plan. Don't be concerned if your list is lengthy; dysfunction is not a permanent condition, but it does develop sequentially if no action is taken to stem its progress.

Developmental Stages of Dysfunction

Everything has a beginning, a place or a point where it started. The same is true for organizations that become dysfunctional—it doesn't happen overnight. Noted author and management theorist Chris Argyris concluded that there are four steps that lead to confusion and chaos. By slightly varying the application, we can use his model to understand how a typical work unit moves through each stage on its way to becoming dysfunctional. While some may reach stage 1 or 2 and remain there, others may move, unchecked, toward stage 3 or 4. If you understand the conditions that define each stage, you may be able to intervene and bring about productive change before the dysfunction sets in permanently.

Stage 1: Ambiguity is not questioned. Say a company directive is somewhat vague, and can logically be interpreted more than one way. Two supervisors interpret the directive differently and give conflicting instructions to employees, not realizing they have countermanded each other. The employees choose not to point this out or ask for clarification. Instead, they follow the directions that suit them best, or they drag their feet until one of the supervisors discovers the ambiguity and provides clarification. The employees do not feel comfortable pointing out an area of potential conflict, even though doing so would relieve their anxiety.

Stage 2: Inconsistencies are ignored. A rule is followed by some and broken by others, but nothing happens to the violators. For example, a group of employees ride together and consistently arrive late for work. Others in the same unit, who travel independently, have been disciplined for not being on time. Attempts to enforce the on-time policy are periodic and lack substance. The inequity is widely known among the staff. When the affected employees finally complain to management, they are told that the issue is being looked into. They are encouraged to mind their own business, and the situation continues, unchanged.

Stage 3: Ambiguities and inconsistencies are undiscussable. It becomes politically incorrect to talk openly about the existence of ambiguity and inconsistency. Should management ask how things could be improved, employees provide shallow responses like, "Well, to tell the truth, the air conditioning doesn't work and there's not enough parking. But don't get me wrong—I *love* it here." People won't risk getting themselves and others into trouble by sharing real issues and telling the truth.

Stage 4: Undiscussability is undiscussable. No one will openly discuss the fact that there *are* serious problems, and that employees are extremely reluctant to discuss them in front of management. Silence during meetings implies not only that problems don't exist, but also that a code of silence should be observed regarding any actions that management might take to address problems. For example, say management conducts an organizationwide climate survey and finds that employee morale and job satisfaction are both low. Shortly after the results are published, the board of directors fires the CEO, three vice presidents, and the human resources manager. Despite the empty seats at the next management meeting, it's business as usual, with nobody mentioning the survey or the purge.

In this day of rapid change and information processing, it is not uncommon for a typical organization to hover between stages 1 and 2 and still remain functional. Signs of more harmful dysfunction begin to appear when the organization settles into stage 3. If stage 4 is reached, the evidence of dysfunction is there, but it is difficult to spot from the inside and therefore more difficult to overcome.

By now you may be ready to assess the level of dysfunction that currently exists in your area of responsibility. Armed with this knowledge, you'll be in a better position to develop a set of management practices that have a three-pronged purpose:

1. To reinforce functional behaviors
2. To discontinue dysfunctional practices
3. To help those in the middle make the right choices

Overcoming dysfunction in the workplace is not *all* doom and gloom. There will of course be some rough times, but for the most part, you'll enjoy seeing employees recognize their dysfunction and openly acknowledge the need to do better. It helps to keep this thought in mind as you work toward functionality in your workplace: Dysfunctional employees are not bad people, they're merely dysfunctional.

2

Closing the Gap

Many of our long-held beliefs about management authority and responsibility evolved in an earlier time, when workers were trained to follow a chain of command. The industrial-era worker labored in an atmosphere of regimentation, structured tasks, and low technology. Supervisors, intolerant of failure, were harsh disciplinarians. This "top-down" system expected managers to direct subordinates in accordance with established procedures, policies, and standards.

In that earlier time, those methods functioned well because uneducated and uninformed workers were conditioned to follow directions without question. Back then, the idea of training employees to respond to a central information source was considered innovative. In other words, our forebears depended on those with authority to take responsibility.

A significant source of dysfunction in today's workplace is managers who can't let go of the command-and-control (or military) model of decision making. This hierarchical, boss-imposed style relies heavily on sole-source, authority-based experts to make judgments as to right and wrong. Similarities can be found in dysfunctional families, where children are subjected to parental decisions that don't make sense. Children from dysfunctional families and employees who work for out-of-touch managers both experience negative consequences without the benefit of understanding cause and effect.

As folks step outside the family to make their way in the world, some take advantage of what they've learned and function successfully in the workplace. Others, however, respond in dysfunctional ways as they struggle to forge work lives for themselves.

Functional employees are "self-responsible" people who know how to state their preferences directly and make accommodations for their own needs. In other words, they have discovered how to gain control and power for themselves. They also have learned to project themselves positively, building and maintaining self-esteem through corrective action. As valued employees, they willingly explore their own roles, responsibilities, and potential contributions to the organization. These employees are intrinsically motivated by a sense of organizational stewardship. They constantly think about ways to improve performance and productivity. It is a privilege and pleasure to work with such people.

Unfortunately, such is not the case with another category of less enthusiastic workers. Exposed to dysfunctional conditions earlier in their lives, these people grew up seeing themselves as victims of restrictive conditioning. They view life as a script that must be followed; in their minds, it cannot be rewritten. Haunted by a fear of failure, they feel powerless to influence what happens to them. They escape judgment by shifting blame and avoiding responsibility. They willingly point out the faults of others, but avoid the truth about their own dysfunctional behaviors and motives.

Dysfunctional employees do only what they have to do to get by. Motivated by extrinsic rewards (pay or promotion), they produce exactly what was agreed upon and no more. Quick to declare, "That's not my job," they prefer narrow boundaries, limited job duties, and minimum complication. Enough of these folks in an organization creates conditions leading to a dysfunctional outcome.

Gaining Acceptance

Bringing functional and dysfunctional employees together to focus on a collective purpose is no easy task. Managers in today's complex organizations are discovering that getting employee groups to develop a common set of goals is not only difficult, but frequently divisive and disruptive to the normal work flow. The challenge is to meld the individual perceptions and expectations into a unified vision.

The primary obstacles keeping employees from coming to a common understanding are most often the variances that exist between their functional and dysfunctional behaviors. For example, functional employees willingly share their viewpoints and eagerly discuss ideas in group meetings. Not so dysfunctional employees, who are suspicious of open deliberations. They either keep quiet or don't respond truthfully in communal settings.

Another major stumbling block to collaboration is getting the dysfunctional employees to accept their share of responsibility. When it comes to accountability, there are two types of employees: those who accept it and those who duck it. Later in this chapter, we'll introduce responsibility charting as a way of tracking who's taking responsibility and who's not. Chances are that it's the dysfunctional employees who are ducking it. If you let them, the functional people will take on more responsibility—they seem to thrive on it. Meanwhile, the dysfunctional folks sit back and enjoy the benefits of someone else's labor, thus splitting the group apart even further.

As these and other behavioral differences are uncovered, some managers simply lay the blame on the dysfunctional workers and try to have them replaced. But ridding the organization of dysfunctional people, even if it were possible, is not the answer. A better solution is to learn how to work with dysfunctional employees. First, it is important to try to understand some of the underlying reasons for dysfunctional behavior. For example, beginning in childhood, dysfunctional employees may have been surrounded by authority figures who have constantly pointed out their faults. Thus, even a well-intentioned exploration of a problem will arouse their instinctive fear of being "found out" and "punished." Or they may suspect that any group assembly is really a disguised attempt to fix the blame and to humiliate those at fault, in which case they may strongly resist self-disclosure in the presence of others. Before they will comfortably participate in the information-sharing process, they will need to appreciate the benefits of mutual discovery.

The more you study workplace behavior, the more you will understand why dysfunctional employees have negative feelings toward group processes. For example, group decision making may remind a dysfunctional employee of the dreaded school playground ritual known as "choosing sides." As a child, this person would give up the chance to join in the game rather than run the risk of not being picked. The same is true when he or she enters the workforce. Fear of rejection is stronger than the desire to participate in group activities.

The opposite is true for functional employees, for whom the opportunity to be part of the group outweighs the risk of rejection. If one group doesn't want them, they find another that does, believing in the adage, "If at first you don't succeed, try, try again." They view groups as positive places for learning about themselves and others, and view peer disapproval as one of the responsibilities of group membership. Functional employees purposely explore relationships to discover how they are perceived by the group. If the group's view is negative, they either work on self-improvement, try to change the group's opinion, or find another group that might appreciate them more.

Clearly, the gap between functional and dysfunctional employees is widening. The rising pressure on employees to "do more with less" will widen it even further in the coming years. Closing that gap is a management responsibility. Spotting it is easy, though, if you know what to look for; it is simply a matter of observing people in action. Next time your group meets, shift the facilitation responsibility to someone else and focus on how each person provides input and gives feedback. The most noteworthy behavioral differences between functional and dysfunctional employees in groups are described in Figure 2-1.

Figure 2-1. Characteristics of employees in groups.

Functional Characteristics	*Dysfunctional Characteristics*
Helping others to understand.	Criticizing others for not understanding.
Sharing beliefs and assumptions.	Telling others what they should do.
Clarifying what is meant.	Challenging what is said.
Being concise and to the point.	Being vague and changing subjects.
Focusing on positive behaviors.	Focusing on negative personalities.
Providing objective descriptions.	Passing subjective judgments.
Opening up to possible change.	Defending the way things are.
Offering studied observations.	Fabricating baseless inferences.
Moving toward the future.	Dwelling on the past.
Providing useful specifics.	Making confusing generalities.

The Group Acceptance Pact

Mainstream management methods can only bridge the gap between functional and dysfunctional employees; bridging, at best, merely provides a communication link between dissociated subgroups. In order to close the gap, you need to conduct a purposeful search for a common meaning without creating intragroup opposition. One way to do this is to form a group acceptance pact (GAP). A GAP is an agreement, preferably in writing, to establish a forum in which group learning and understanding are sought, judgment is suspended, and agreement is not necessary. Acceptance is a critical factor in getting dysfunctional employees to broaden their expectations enough to feel secure in a group. Dysfunctional employees are more likely to acknowledge the views of others if they are first accepted "as is" and not pressured to change as a condition of belonging.

The group acceptance pact is simple to design. The following guidelines will help provide dysfunctional employees an opportunity to practice self-responsibility in the safety of a mutually supportive group environment:

Keep Focused

- Stick to the agenda.
- Don't bring up unrelated issues.
- Talk about one issue at a time.
- Fully explore each item before moving on.

Speak Without Blame

- Share only what you know firsthand.
- Be truthful about what happened.
- Avoid faultfinding.
- Seek all the facts.

Comment Without Judgment

- Listen to all ideas, thoughts, and recommendations.
- Resist speaking against or in support of suggestions.
- Refrain from using gestures to express your concerns.
- Don't try to explain one person's thoughts to another.

Set Aside Attachments

- Avoid aligning yourself in advance of the meeting.
- Be open to all outcomes and possibilities during the meeting.
- Leave your personal agenda outside until after the meeting.
- Don't lobby others to support your position during the meeting.

Search for Meaning

- Provide explanations as often as requested.
- Encourage comments, questions, and clarifications.
- Look for the best in whatever is said.
- Ask for examples of how things might work.

Acknowledge Others

- ⋆ Encourage silent members to provide input.
- ⋆ Pay attention to each person as he or she speaks.
- ⋆ Observe a short pause after each speaker is finished.
- ⋆ Repeat what has been said to let others know they were heard.

Participate Fully

- ⋆ Avoid side comments and conversations.
- ⋆ Don't interrupt the person talking.
- ⋆ Take frequent breaks to keep everyone fresh.
- ⋆ Restrict outside telephone calls and messages.

Trust the Process

- ⋆ Don't suggest changing the process once it's begun.
- ⋆ If the process isn't working, look to the group for answers.
- ⋆ Ask others how they feel about the way things are going.
- ⋆ Discuss why you feel the process isn't working.

Managers who have used the GAP have discovered that it greatly enhances the acceptance and implementation of team building, joint decision making, group problem solving, and collaborative conflict resolution between and among functional and dysfunctional employees. The biggest payoff comes when dysfunctional employees practice self-disclosure and are no longer dependent upon management for guidance. By practicing self-disclosure in the security of the GAP, they have become self-directed problem solvers who can think for themselves.

Now that you've armed them with a new set of skills, it's time for the dysfunctional employees to take on more responsibility. A more equitable distribution of accountability will lead to higher levels of performance. Shifting the responsibility will also bring more balance to the team and strengthen their working relationships.

Responsibility Charting

Anyone responsible for producing results is keenly aware of the mounting problems facing today's leaders. Managers in every field of endeavor are discovering that the responsibility for getting things done keeps floating back up the chain of command. This newly emerging phenomenon is called *upward delegation.* Upward delegation is at work when dysfunctional subordinates, hoping to avoid the consequences of being wrong, repeatedly send issues back up the chain of command, requesting more information each time, until management runs out of patience and makes the decision. In the group version, called *unless otherwise directed,* subordinates offer to make decisions—but let it be known that they're willing to change if you say so. If you let it stand and it works, the group takes the credit. Should it fail, well, you didn't direct otherwise, so you're held accountable.

Instead of accepting responsibility for an unsatisfactory outcome, dysfunctional employees tend to blame each other for what went wrong. Managers, tired of playing these games, are less likely to delegate decision making and problem solving to groups, preferring instead to manage the functional employees one-on-one and leave the dysfunctional ones to themselves. At first glance, this may seem to resolve the dilemma, but in reality it adds to the dysfunction. Besides, any time you may save will later be eaten up by individual complaints from dysfunctional employees who think you're playing favorites. Fortunately, there is a better way to handle the problem.

Andrew S. Grove, Intel's founding father, emphasized the importance of bringing key people together in groups when he said, "Meetings are the medium through which management occurs." If you're like most managers, meetings are the primary setting in which to discuss roles, relationships, and responsibilities. In other words, they are the place where all your people get to see you in action. Therefore, this precious opportunity must be fruitful and productive for everyone who attends.

In *Designing Complex Organizations,* Jay R. Galbraith introduces us to responsibility charting as a way "to clarify and shape the structure to fit the participants and their work." This easy-to-use process identifies the "various tasks of a work unit and provides a language for pinpointing authority, roles, and reporting relationships." Responsibility charting enables an organization to talk about structure by breaking it down into specific functions and tasks. Managers find it particularly helpful when launching a new venture or getting a floundering project back on track.

Take a minute to scan Figure 2-2. Notice that a matrix is formed: The names of the people involved are written across the top (horizontal) row, and the various tasks are listed in order along the side in the first (vertical) column. Also note that in the column beneath each person's name, letters ap-

Figure 2-2. Responsibility charting.

	TOM	ALICE	BOB	JOHN	MARY	SUE		
Task #1	C	R	A	C	I	I		
Task #2	I	C	A	C	I	R		
Task #3	R	I	A	C	I	C		
Task #4	I	C	A	C	R	I		
Task #5								
Task #6								
Task #7								
Task #8								

pear. The letters, **R**, **A**, **C**, and **I**, represent the roles that are to be performed for each task. Each of the four key identification letters has a different meaning.

R *Responsibility.* The person accountable for taking action.

A *Approve.* The person whose approval is needed before action is taken.

C *Consult.* The person(s) to be consulted while the action is being taken.

I *Inform.* The person(s) to be informed when the action is complete.

First, let's go over the mechanics of the responsibility charting process, or RACI for short. Then we'll walk through some real examples of how the process works. For the sake of simplicity, Figure 2-2 depicts a small number of fictitious names and a set of tasks numbered 1 to 8. Your chart would include a definitive description for each task and indicate the actual people involved by name or by position. If you had committees, advisory groups, task forces, a board of directors, or other standing bodies, they would also be listed on the top horizontal row and assigned an identifying letter according to their function(s).

As a general rule, there is only one **R** for each task. The person with the **R** should understand and accept the conditions of performance, which may include budget, time frame, completion dates, and milestones. (As tempting as it might be, it is not a good idea to give someone the **R** as punishment for not showing up at the first meeting.) Our example shows that for Task 1, Alice has the **R**, meaning that she is responsible for taking action.

For Task 1, Bob has the designation **A**, meaning that he must give the final approval or authorization. This makes it clear that before final action is taken, Alice needs to run it by Bob to get his approval. Alice will coordinate with Bob just how far she can go on her own before Bob needs to get involved.

Tom and John are both assigned the **C** role on Task 1. The **C** indicates that a certain level of expertise is necessary for the successful completion of the task and lets Alice know that she must consult with both Tom and John as the task progresses.

It's important to note that only those persons designated **R** and **C** need to attend the Task 1 meetings—a time saver for everyone. The **A** person may want to show up just prior to the launch to acknowledge people for doing a good job. The **I** persons (in this example, Mary and Sue) don't need to attend task meetings because Alice **(R)** is keeping them informed as the task progresses. When Task 1 reaches the point where Task 2 needs to be started, Sue will be up to speed and ready to don the **R** hat to get Task 2 under way. Notice that each **I** in our example assumes the **R** role for a subsequent task.

In addition to keeping track of the status of each task within a project, the RACI can be used to evaluate the contribution of each player. For example, John has had the **C** role on all four tasks. He could be ready to assume the **R** role on Task 5. This is a good way to shift responsibility to those who are ready. It also provides a record of work flow for each task within a given project.*

Putting the Pieces Together

Responsibility charting has been used successfully in a variety of situations. The following case shows how RACI was applied in a large, nonprofit system.

Several years ago a nationwide renewal of spiritual faith and religious practices began. Attendance at mainstream churches surged. For some churches this influx of worshipers was a welcome sight, but not so for the institution in our story. What at first looked like a blessing soon turned into a burden. As the numbers of worshipers increased, the church administration was stretched beyond its ability. The need for additional services and new facilities overtaxed its best efforts.

Unlike many other churches, its problem was not a lack of funds,

*Jay R. Galbraith, *Designing Complex Organizations* (Reading, Mass.: Addison Wesley Longman, 1973), pp. 146–148. © Copyright 1973 Addison Wesley Longman, Inc. Reprinted by permission of Addison Wesley Longman.

since increased giving matched the rise in attendance. Surprisingly, the hottest issue was how to integrate the newcomers into the life of the church without alienating the existing congregation. Many of the long-standing members felt that this rush to find religion would fade, and fought vehemently against building new facilities and adding new staff.

The governing board soon found itself embroiled in heated debates over how to park the cars and seat the crowds on Sundays. Struggles broke out between the "new blood" and the "old guard" over the worship, education, and music programs. Frustrated with the status quo, some of the new members organized their own Bible study groups. The volunteer choir erupted when the new director held auditions and bypassed several singers who had been members for years. The list went on.

I was brought in just as the governing board was deciding what to do about the senior pastor's pay raise, which was overdue. Denomination bylaws required a performance review plus a congregational vote of approval before a pay raise could be granted, and the board members were concerned that polling the membership at this tender moment might further divide the church. They also felt that postponing the review would buy them time to address the mounting dysfunction.

A careful examination of the activities assigned to the ministerial staff, the church committees, and the governing board was matched against a survey of new member expectations. This effort produced a list of sixteen distinct functions.

Control over these functions turned out to be the primary source of strife and discord between the ministerial staff and the governing board, with the church office often caught in the middle. Apparently, this hadn't been a problem when the church was smaller. In the words of one long-standing board member, "We used to trust each other to do the right thing." Evidently, as the church grew, so did the misunderstandings and misgivings.

Using the RACI process, it took about six months of concentrated effort to work through the authority and responsibility issues for all sixteen functions. A review of the completed charts revealed that a handful of long-time members had the **R** on most of the committees. Coincidentally, these committees were the main sources of conflict and controversy. The charting process also pointed out openings on committees where new members could be plugged in. Finding volunteers to fill the vacancies was easy, but getting the faithful to let go of their committee assignments presented a problem.

Not wanting to single out or offend anyone, the governing board came up with an ingenious plan to reorganize the committee system. It proposed that all committee business be conducted at the church on the same night each month. Those serving on multiple committees were asked to stay with one and resign from the others; the resulting vacancies were immediately filled by new members. Meeting on the same night gave committees the opportunity to share information and consult with one another. The governing board was on hand to review and approve recommendations. As more members got involved in the business of the church, issues that might have divided them actually brought them together.

Role Confusion

In the previous example, the RACI was applied in a formal manner. Actual charts were created, and written documents were produced and placed in binders for frequent review to confirm or clarify responsibilities. This more exacting style is used in larger, more complex systems, where people may not get together very often. In a small group or single team setting, a simpler, more informal version often makes more sense.

Instead of creating a written chart, "hats" are used to indicate who's performing what role. For example, let's say you're discussing a sticky situation with your team when someone asks, "If you were me, what would you do?" As people listen to your reply, some interpret what you say as an order because they see you as wearing an **A** hat. Others might see an **I** hat and figure that you're just making a comment. This is often referred to as role confusion.

The more informal the setting, the more likely it is that someone will get confused when you switch hats. Role confusion contributes to dysfunction because it creates ambiguity and inconsistency. In this case it's not a gap between functional and dysfunctional employees but a lack of clarity on your part. Until people get used to the RACI process, the best way to prevent role confusion is to declare what role you're filling each time you speak. Let people know that you will be changing roles and that if they get confused, it's okay to ask what hat you're wearing.

Organizational needs have changed; so must leadership skills. Traditional methods put too great an emphasis on management knowledge, expertise, and experience. Managers now need to recognize and accept that they can accomplish far more by sharing responsibility than by working alone. A collaborative information-sharing process like responsibility charting empowers employees while infusing new energy throughout the workplace.

The modern company needs people who can cope with reduced planning cycles, new realities, and multiple opportunities in a constantly changing environment. In order to better solve problems, people at all levels must learn to take responsibility and collaborate in the planning and decision-making processes. To be effective, employees must learn to be their own experts.

As workers learn to rely less on what you might know and focus more on taking responsibility, you'll find they will be making better decisions. And before long they'll be working together to overcome whatever dysfunction turns up in their workplace.

3

Solving Problems

At a recent team-building seminar, a weary manager complained that getting employees involved in solving problems was like trying to keep a beach ball under water: "Every time you let go, it pops back to the surface." Another manager confessed that a problem in her company didn't get resolved because an employee claimed he "couldn't get a handle on it." It appears that in some of today's pressure-packed workplaces, when managers try to empower subordinates to resolve problems on their own, the response is too frequently, "That's not my job."

Scenarios like these could be a sign that you're working in a dysfunctional organization, or you could be surrounded by people who lack the confidence to solve problems on their own, or there could be a mixture of both. We'll have more to say about working in a dysfunctional setting later; for now, let's concentrate on getting those around you to become a little more self-directed when it comes to solving problems.

If you decide to take on this challenge, it's important to be patient. It also helps to understand and accept that dysfunctional employees are not willing to tackle a problem unless they are confident of a positive result. Dysfunctional employees view problem solving as a high-risk situation that could get them in trouble or even jeopardize their jobs. Unlike functional employees, who seek opportunities for advancement and recognition, these folks maintain a low profile and try not to rock the boat. If they do take on a problem, they want to be left alone to resolve it in a way that makes sense to them. Any pressure from above to meet deadlines or provide feedback is liable to be greeted with a scowl and a caustic comment like "Quit breathing down my neck" or "Get off my back."

Such behavior is dysfunctional, and it is more common than you might think. Business consultant and author Ferdinand F. Fournies conducted a fifteen-year study of why employees failed to resolve problems on their own. In his book *Why Employees Don't Do What They're Supposed to Do and What to Do About It,* Fournies makes the point that "getting employees to do what they are supposed to do is probably the biggest challenge for any manager." Researchers like Fournies have clearly shown us that when an employee fails, so does the manager. If that's the case, then managers also reap the benefits when dysfunctional employees become effective problem solvers.

Most managers have the basic skills necessary to survive and even excel in their present roles. It seems to me that passing some of these skills along to the dysfunctional employees would help them both. The next step, then, is to look for opportunities where this could happen in your workplace.

Plugging People In

In a dysfunctional organization, the problem-solving process falls into a predictable pattern. First, the manager recognizes a problem, investigates the cause, and decides on a solution. Next, the remedy is handed over to a subordinate, who is expected to make it work. Since that person lacks the necessary background information, the decisions she or he makes while implementing the manager's solution often make the problem worse. The employee gets blamed for the failure, but has no idea what went wrong or what to do to change the outcome.

If this sounds familiar to you, then maybe it's time to try something else.

A dysfunctional work unit is a strong indicator that its members are not functioning well as individuals, either. In order to change their behavior, you might consider changing what *you* do. For a start, become less of an adjudicator. Being the one with the right answers may make you feel good, but it doesn't help them learn to solve things on their own.

When functional employees resolve an issue, the resolution belongs to them. They take ownership of it and care about the results. Dysfunctional employees, on the other hand, have no confidence in solutions suggested to them by others. Since they usually have little or nothing invested in someone else's solution, there is little for them to care about. They expect someone with authority to keep tabs on the situation, and step in if problems resurface.

Rather than solve their problems for them, your role is to get dysfunctional people to engage in the process. The challenge is to create an atmosphere of understanding, awareness, and perspective by getting them to focus on solutions to current problems. They may need your help if they become preoccupied with what went wrong. Be persistent in directing their energy toward what's facing them now. Try posing future-focused questions like, "How do we avoid this next time?" "How should we do it differently?" "If you were in charge, how would you meet this challenge?" "What resources do you need?" "What do you want from me?"

In order for dysfunctional employees to become functional problem solvers, they'll need more help than they've been getting. The following is a short list of their immediate needs:

* To find a richer variety of resources for comparison
* To learn how to seek help from others
* To appreciate the value of teamwork
* To be encouraged, especially when they fail
* To realize there's at least one solution to every problem

Since most of these needs are beyond the scope of mainstream educational programs, it looks like it's up to you to provide the necessary training. The tools and techniques presented here should help you get started.

Dealing With Problems

Most managers have a set way of dealing with problems. Your technique most likely depends on the nature of the issue, the urgency of resolving it, and the availability of information. Once you've assessed these factors, you can then decide to solve the problem yourself, bring in a colleague, or delegate it to a subordinate. The first two choices are the easiest of the three. It's the decision to delegate that sometimes gets sticky.

We all have our favorite employees—the ones who don't complain when we hand them a task. Then there are the not-so-favorites who reach for the grievance list when they see us heading their way. Well, as tempting as it might be to stay with the former, it's time for you to do otherwise. A functional workplace is one in which all employees participate fully in problem-solving processes, and this can't happen if you continue to look to the same few people for solutions.

Next time you've got a problem that needs to be delegated, bring in one of your less favored employees and introduce the four-step process outlined below. This technique is designed to inspire dysfunctional employees to settle their own issues and thus free high achievers for more rewarding and challenging tasks.

1. *Identify the cause.* What created the deviation from expectations?
   Define precisely what went wrong.
   Gather information on what, where, when, and how it happened.
   Explore the factors that might have triggered the deviation.
   Select the most likely cause for the deviation.
   Test assumptions—is the problem likely to recur?
2. *Select the solution.* What action should be taken?
   Determine who "owns" the problem.
   Define the desired results.
   Generate a list of workable options in priority order.
   Invite input from those affected by the alternatives.
   Pick the solution that is most likely to work.

3. *Implement the resolution.* What might prevent a successful outcome?
   Seek out possible opposition to the action plan.
   Brainstorm potential threats to the decision.
   Determine the severity of each threat.
   Estimate the probability of a negative outcome.
   Clarify authority, responsibility, and reporting relationships.
4. *Evaluate the result.* What happened? Did the solution work?
   Set time lines and measurements.
   Establish negative and positive incentives for compliance.
   Make sure that appropriate action was taken.
   Follow up to see if the problem was resolved.
   Record the results.

The element of the four-step process that is most often overlooked is the evaluation in step 4. Too often, once a solution has been implemented, it is assumed that it has worked. So if it fails, no one says anything. In fact, dysfunctional employees distance themselves from these unsolved problems because they don't want to be in range when the "stuff hits the fan."

The process as outlined can be effective only when all four steps are followed, so it is important for those being trained to know where and when they're being plugged into the process. For example, a manager spots a problem and assigns an employee to begin an investigation into its cause. Even though a solution might be obvious, the manager might tell the employee to hold off taking any action until a list of all possible causes has been identified. The manager and the employee then review the list and together decide which cause makes the most sense.

Another scenario might be that the cause has been identified by an employee, who takes it to the manager for a remedy. The manager asks the employee to come up with a prioritized list of solutions, and they go over the list to decide if the employee or some other person will be responsible for implementation.

At first, the employees you're training may reject the process because they fear making mistakes. They'll be expecting you to make a big deal of it if failure does occur—so don't. In order to gain confidence in the four-step process, dysfunctional employees need opportunities to start over, without penalty, should their first solution turn out to be a dud. The axiom, "If at first you don't succeed, try, try again," assumes that there's no punishment for failure. When dysfunctional employees are encouraged to pick up the pieces and try again, they begin to trust the process and ultimately themselves. Once they have the four steps firmly in mind, they will understand where and when to plug themselves into the process.

When these folks are comfortable working through the four-step process on their own, it's time for them to solve problems collectively. Even though they may be confident working with you, they may be reluctant to demonstrate their newly acquired skills in the presence of their coworkers. Solving problems in a group context can sometimes be chaotic and confusing, especially to someone who prefers to work alone.

Working in a State of Confusion

Some of us learned early in life to avoid confusion, or at least not to admit to it, even when it was painfully obvious that we didn't know what to do. It seemed that every time we thought we understood the rules of a game, the game was changed and the old rules were tossed out. As we grew up and the problems got more complex and harder to solve on our own, we naturally turned to our parents and teachers for help.

Sometimes we got understanding, sympathy, and sage advice. Other times our elders were simply amused by our struggle. Occasionally we were subjected to tiresome scoldings, reprimands, and critical assessments. Not only did our self-confidence take a big hit, but we probably came away feeling belittled, embarrassed, and more confused than before.

Given this all-too-common background, it's no wonder that so many people in today's workforce don't function well when they are confused. Yet in order to successfully keep up with the pace of change, a state of confusion is exactly what managers must force themselves, and their employees, to endure.

A note of caution: As you begin to explore working in a state of confusion, remember that you are dealing with deeply held feelings, perceptions, and fears—including your own. Although people can cover up their fears or hold them in check when things are going well, these fears often crop up when a situation is less clear-cut. When pushed to respond to ambiguity and inconsistency, dysfunctional employees are reluctant to act, thinking that their inadequacies will be exposed. It is up to you to create a safe learning environment in which these employees can express themselves without fear of exposure and admonition. The state of confusion is a facilitated group process designed to bring people together to uncover facts rather than point out faults.

Webster's New World Dictionary defines *confusion* as "the act of confusing, or the state of disarray; disorder; perplexity of the mind; or embarrassment." Given that definition, you might be wondering why you would intentionally create such a state. There's a very good reason: When people are confused, they are susceptible to redirection and open to new information. What better time could there be to relieve their anxiety and discomfort? If you can do that in a group setting, think of the possible benefits.

Stick with this thought for a while longer and hopefully you'll feel differently about confusion. Let's start with a more constructive definition. If you take a closer look in the dictionary, you'll see that *con* also means "to study carefully" and *fusion* means "blending together." So, if you think of *confusion* using a constructive mind-set, it can take on a useful, positive meaning: to study or learn together. A loose interpretation might be the *joining of thoughts,* or what Mr. Spock on *Star Trek* called a "mind meld." After an encounter with Spock, people were no longer confused; they had been enlightened by their exposure to his superior intellect. You can accomplish the same thing by blending together the thinking power in your team.

A state of confusion is most likely to occur when a situation, a circumstance, or an event forces people to work on an unfamiliar problem together. It is very likely that some type of organizational change is the driving force stirring up the problem. A new set of problems creates confusion because it alters what people are used to doing. Also, new problems force people to work in unfamiliar ways, sometimes with people they don't trust or don't like. When faced with new problems, dysfunctional employees want to be left alone and have everything remain as is: predictable, definable, and within their limited control. Getting used to new things and new people is not to their liking. Dysfunctional employees are known to have narrow comfort zones and are often confounded by uncertainty.

The Three Pathways

The model shown in Figure 3-1 was developed through a series of close observations and interviews with employees who admitted to being confused. The model is based on detailed interviews with hundreds of employees from more than 200 organizations over a period of fifteen years. A careful study of the findings revealed several commonalities. These similar experiences provide the basis for the notion that there are definable or descriptive categories present in a state of confu-

Figure 3-1. State of confusion.

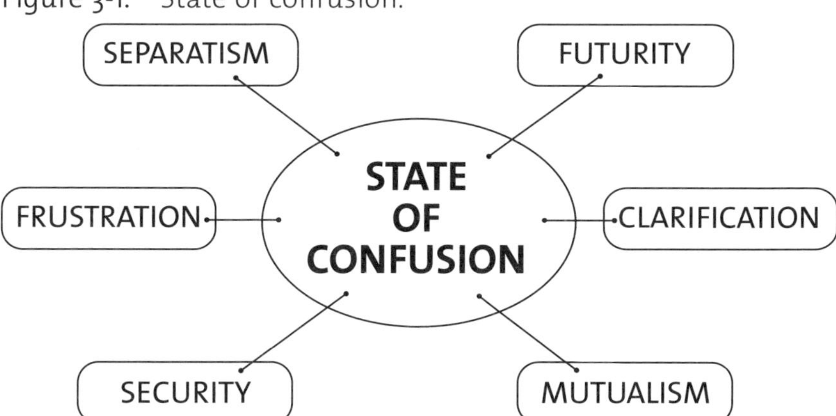

sion. Each of these takes the form of a path that shows the way without disclosing what's at the end. (It's like going up a mountain trail. Although you are not familiar with the route, you can tell that others have been this way before, so you assume it's okay to follow.)

Figure 3-1 provides a visual interpretation of the three pathways that come together to form a state of confusion. Each has two opposite extremes. As employees travel along, they are likely to experience confusion at various points along the way. Your challenge is to keep them moving until they reach the functional end of each course.

As you review the descriptions of these pathways, note that the pathways are progressive and tend to follow the first three stages of dysfunction (see Chapter 1). There is no parallel with the fourth stage or dysfunction in the state of confusion model because by that stage most of the functional people have left or are looking for another job, while the dysfunctional folks have reached such a high level of apathy that nothing matters other than their own survival.

Separatism–Mutualism

Ambiguity at the first stage of dysfunction strongly affects the *separatism–mutualism* pathway. When policies are vague and individuals consequently receive conflicting directions from their supervisors, they start to get anxious about failure. As being right becomes more difficult, it seems safer to wait and do nothing than to risk being wrong. They notice that when some people solve problems their own way, nothing is said, but others are disciplined for not following directions. Dysfunctional employees will not be comfortable pointing out these inconsistencies. If the ambiguities are not challenged by someone else and subsequently clarified, they will occur more frequently. This sets the stage for the next level of dysfunction.

The differences between separatism (dysfunctional) and mutualism (functional) behaviors at this first stage are subtle and not easy to spot. However, there are two critical factors. First, the dysfunctional folks move away from problems and pull away from the group. Second, functional people move toward a problem and look to the group for answers. The following list provides a sampling of both types of behavior. When they are viewed together, the contrasts are more noticeable.

Separatism

* Myopic self-interest—single-focused, individual viewpoints are held.
* Job descriptions and work assignments are not followed.
* Problems are passed up the chain of command.

Mutualism

* Enlightened—group perspectives and opinions are openly shared.
* Self-directed teams establish goals and set priorities.
* Constant improvement is expected and realized quickly.

These contrasting behaviors may at first appear to be a normal, natural part of everyday work life, which they are. However, if you expect people with differing work habits to join together when they are confused, it's not likely to happen without your involvement.

The dysfunctional behaviors checklist would make a great discussion starter, as would the functional/dysfunctional characteristics list or the group acceptance pact. Later, the responsibility chart could be used to keep the group from advancing to the next stage of dysfunction.

Frustration–Clarification

The fact that inconsistencies are ignored is the hallmark of the second stage of dysfunction. This typically coincides with movement along the *frustration–clarification* pathway. Dysfunctional employees are no strangers to disappointment and dissatisfaction; they tend to get used to them. But when rules are relaxed for some people and not for others, these employees begin to worry that management has a hidden agenda—especially when they don't know what's acceptable and what's not. If managers are aware of what's going on, they may try to explain the contradictions and mixed messages. However, if inconsistencies persist, dysfunctional employees will begin to feed their frustrations into the rumor mill, opening the gate to the next level of dysfunction.

Unlike the contrasts between the behaviors in the previous stage, the differences between the two extremes are harder to notice. There is, however, one observable characteristic that sets the dysfunctional and functional employees apart. The functional folks will express their frustration and ask for clarification in the same statement, making it easy for you to connect the two. While this is going on, the dysfunctional people will sit quietly, nodding or shaking their heads to show agreement or disagreement, respectively. By comparing the following list, you can see some of these behaviors lurking just below the surface.

Frustration

* Disappointment, disillusionment, and dissatisfaction with the way things are
* Hindrances to completion of work
* Unstated expectations, hidden agendas, contradictions, and mixed messages

Clarification

* Reflection, understanding, awareness, and discovery
* Stated expectations plus formally acknowledged purpose
* Hopeful perspectives and a greater sense of connection

With a little practice you'll be able to dig out the frustrations of dysfunctional employees and get these employees working alongside the functional folks. The behaviors listed above seem natural to both the functional and dysfunctional employees. Your challenge at this stage is to put a stop to the dysfunctional practices by reinforcing the functional ones.

This would be a good time to adopt the four-step problem-solving model as a group process. Inserting the responsibility charting process would be a good idea and may prevent the group from progressing to stage 3.

Security–Futurity

Once the third stage of dysfunction has been reached, it is very likely that the dysfunctional and functional employees are firmly entrenched at opposite ends of the *security–futurity* pathway. By now it has become politically incorrect to speak openly about the existence of ambiguity and inconsistency. Dysfunctional employees will believe that it's unwise to share their concerns with anyone in management. They will keep to themselves and work silently to uphold the status quo. Their overall resistance to the group process is likely to get stronger unless you give them no choice.

At this stage, the functional employees are looking to the future and the dysfunctional employees are holding on to the past. Pulling both types together in a state of confusion produces one immediate benefit: It forces everyone to concentrate on the same issues at the same time. When you review the list below, you gain perspective on just how far apart these folks are.

Security

- Predictable environment, clear goals, firm future, slow growth, no changes
- Secure job with a promising outlook
- Steady work flow, higher pay, regular promotions

Futurity

- Flexible, fluid, and free-flowing
- Open to job changes, advanced technology, and new work methods
- Confident that positions exist for those willing to move into the future

Once you get the dysfunctional people to open up in a group setting, your challenge will be to keep them from digging up the past. It's good for them to share their concerns and for you to hear what's behind their confusion, but, if you're not careful, this can turn into a therapeutic story-telling session in which they rationalize their behavior. If you feel the need for such a session, that's fine; just understand that while the dysfunctional employees are likely to leave the gathering with a little less guilt and decreased apprehensions, they'll have no further insight into what needs to happen next. And worse yet, they'll still be confused.

The responsibility charting process is a good way to get them to focus less on their own issues and more on the problems facing the group. The group acceptance pact and the four-step model are both useful at this stage. Whatever you do is bound to be helpful and should keep them from becoming more dysfunctional.

Keeping Track of Progress

No matter which pathway you're working on, the group's progress will still be influenced by individual reactions to changing situations in their workplace. In other words, whatever is going on around these folks will be reflected in what they say and do when they get confused. This is all the more reason to keep track of the progress they're making and point it out at the beginning of each session.

Although these folks will still get confused from time to time, thanks to your efforts they'll know how to work their way through their confusion. This is truly good news. It means that all of your people will understand what you're trying to do and eagerly join in because it feels natural to them.

Once you've successfully engaged the brain power of your dysfunctional employees, you will notice a remarkable change in the workplace. Involving them in the search for solutions will have beefed up their confidence. They'll discover that satisfying resolutions lead to a satisfying work life. And when they are faced with a problem, instead of letting it fester or passing it off to someone else, they'll look for opportunities to solve it. As a result, their natural curiosity will be maintained, and their self-confidence sustained.

4

Making Teams Work

Teamwork has become a growth industry in this country. Almost every management guru has written a book selling corporate America on the notion that quality and service can be improved by forming people into teams. Corporate America has bought in to the notion in a very big way: Since the introduction of quality circles at Lockheed in 1973, employers have spent billions of dollars on training programs, seminars, workshops, books, audiocassettes, and videos promoting teamwork.

So you'd think that by now, teamwork would have a positive track record and a firm hold on our corporate culture. Not so! University of Southern California management professor Edward Lawler oversaw a survey that revealed that 68 percent of the *Fortune* 1,000 companies use self-managed or high-performance teams. While this may sound like a lot, that same study showed that only 10 percent of workers actually work in teams.

What's happened? Why isn't the team concept having more of an impact? "People are very naïve about how easy it is to create a team," explains Lawler. Employers assume that employees know how to work together. That's an erroneous assumption. People *don't* know how to work together; it's something they've never been taught.

Teaching takes place in two key locations: at school and at home. For more than 100 years, young people have been subjected to teaching and parenting methods designed to prepare them to work in an industrial-based society. Times have changed, but our school-family systems have not. They simply are not providing the kind of worker needed in today's fast-paced, multitasked, team-focused workplace. A brief look at our school-family system will help you understand why.

School-Family Systems

Reformers suggest that our school-family (education) systems are dysfunctional and, at the very least, in need of a drastic overhaul. One reason for this widespread dysfunction is the model that these systems are still using.

The mission of the industrial-era school-family system was to train students to compete with one another for the approval of teachers, parents, and employers. Good grades in school led to approval at home, which became the measure of how children achieved recognition and value. The school-family system reinforced the belief that success is based upon sustained individual achievement, measured by one's ability to outperform others.

Competition in our education system, coupled with sibling rivalry at home, has created an environment of myopic self-interest. Students are tested individually under strict supervision. Upon leaving school, they seek a good-paying job with benefits and opportunities for advancement. They enter the labor force valuing only what they know and what they can do for themselves—working with others is not important. Such employees are likely to block or resist team building because being part of a team is not a priority. After all, they've been taught that trading information with one's peers is called cheating. As far back as they can remember, anyone caught collaborating, other than in extracurricular activities, suffered negative consequences both at school and at home. In today's terms, this attitude is dysfunctional. Modern employers expect employees to participate collectively in the problem-solving process.

Tenets of Teamwork

If you're a manager trying to build a team, you have a difficult task ahead of you. The first challenge is to understand the difference between *building a team* and *forming a group*. If your employees have been working together for some time, the chances are that they have already formed a group, or at least assumed some of the characteristics of a group. Since the characteristics of a group are not the same as those of a team, you may need to sell your employees on the advantages of re-forming the group into a team.

Marvin E. Shaw, in his book *Group Dynamics: The Psychology of Small Group Behavior*, identified six characteristics that define a group:*

1. *Perception.* Members can identify who else is in the group.
2. *Motivation.* Members feel rewarded by belonging to the group.
3. *Goals.* Members work together for an agreed-upon purpose.
4. *Organization.* Members know what role they play in the group.
5. *Interdependency.* Members rely on one another to achieve the goal.
6. *Interaction.* Members communicate face-to-face with one another.

So how does a group differ from a team? The most noteworthy distinction is the way differences are handled. Groups tend to follow the school-family system prescription for indi-

*Marvin E. Shaw, Group Dynamics: The Psychology of Small Group Behavior (New York: McGraw-Hill, 1981). Reproduced with permission of the McGraw-Hill Companies.

vidual socialization. That is, they impose restrictions on individuality. Although groups develop their own norms, they tend to adhere to primary societal injunctions such as, *To get along, go along. Don't rock the boat. The majority rules.* Groups rarely encourage creative thinking. Instead, they follow established policies, standards, and procedures without question. Loyalty is demanded of all members, and those who fail to follow the rules are expelled from the group.

Because groups thrive on conformity, they do not deal with the causes of conflict. When conflict arises, the majority view prevails. This rigidity or nonacceptance of differing viewpoints may cause the opposition to split off and form a separate group. In the workplace, such splintering creates additional barriers for the manager, who now must contend with rival groups that have opposing goals.

Breaking down these barriers requires the introduction of a new ideology—a set of guiding principles upon which team spirit can be built. The five *tenets of teamwork* shown in Figure 4-1 provide an effective structure within which people can work together cooperatively. As a manager, you can use these tenets as a tool to evaluate the results of team building between and within work units. It is important to note that

Figure 4-1. Tenets of teamwork.

- *MUTUAL RESPECT*
- *COMMON PURPOSE*
- *PRODUCTIVE COMMUNICATION*
- *DESIRE TO WORK TOGETHER*
- *NEUTRAL ENVIRONMENT*

team building will not be effective until all of these tenets are developed.

Mutual Respect

Team members need to accept one another as individuals.

* All members are viewed as equal contributors, and individuals are not encouraged by management to change the views and values of others on the team.
* Expectations are developed and shared between team members before action is taken.
* If team objectives are not met, the team focuses on clarification and correction rather than on faultfinding and blaming.
* Team members do not have to like one another, but they must accept one another as is!

Common Purpose

Team members need to work toward the same things at the same time.

* Time and energy must be spent deciding on a joint purpose. The purpose often changes during interactions among team members. All changes must be identified and discussed before the team continues its work.
* Some team members will want to look at problems to find out what went wrong, while others will choose to focus on what needs to be done differently. Both functions are equally important. Often both must be applied simultaneously.
* Team leadership is charged with the responsibility of guiding the problem-solving and decision-making process so that all team members are cognizant of it.

Productive Communication

Organizational and interpersonal communication, written or verbal, must focus on producing results.

- Communication among individual team members should move the team forward toward mutually acceptable outcomes.
- Team members must come away from meetings and one-on-one interactions understanding not only what was communicated, but also what was meant and what action they are expected to take.
- Team members need to establish a task-analysis process to clarify the responsibilities governing the structure of each work unit.
- The team needs to review its authority, roles, and reporting relationships prior to taking action.

Desire to Work Together

Team members need to help one another to understand that they can accomplish more by working together than by working alone.

- The organization's promotional and reward systems must support this concept by recognizing and supporting team efforts.
- The performance and productivity system may also need to be realigned to record collective accomplishments. Individual achievers need to believe that they don't have to give up something in order to become team members.
- The team needs to identify ways in which coworkers can contribute to the accomplishment of team goals. A collaborative spirit will develop as members gain confidence in the other members' commitment to the team.

Neutral Environment

The team must accept that occasional conflicts between individuals are normal, and can provide a natural opportunity for creativity.

- The team must develop a process that recognizes conflicts when they occur and brings them into the open for discussion. Such a process should include both the identification of the cause of the conflict and the development of a resolution that can be supported by all members of the team.

* Effective teams learn how to resolve their differences quickly. If the team cannot resolve individual disagreements, then the affected members must set aside their conflict and not allow it to block teamwork.

Team Building

The ultimate goal of building a team is to provide the members with the ability to sustain a high level of success and to perform as a cohesive unit while taking greatest advantage of their eagerness to succeed as individuals. This is usually accomplished by using a two-pronged approach: (1) provide each team with the tools and techniques it needs to get the job done, and (2) provide team members with the ability to make a personal impact on the way their team performs.

As a manager, your role in team building is to serve as a catalyst that helps different and complex people get along in the workplace. You are not a disciplinarian or a magician, making a team appear where there wasn't one before. Instead, your job is to help to create an atmosphere of respect and acceptance. People still have to make the adjustments, and the process is always far from textbook. Every team is unique in its combination of individuals.

A successful team-building program should convert the workplace into an environment in which each team member is afforded the opportunity to:

* Understand and be motivated to accomplish the goals of the team.
* Gain insights into the beliefs and values of other team members.
* Increase participation, build self-confidence, and gain credibility.

* Distinguish between work-performance and work-behavioral problems.
* Use personal skills to develop a sense of responsibility.
* Identify the human factors coworkers need to do a good job.
* Think positively about changing unproductive behaviors.
* Understand failure better and accept criticism.
* Develop a more cooperative atmosphere in interpersonal relations.

Effective team building will produce a unified, cohesive unit of employees who appreciate one another's special functions and know how to support one another to get the job done. Don't forget that the goal of team building is not to construct new individuals out of old ones, but to build trust among people so that collaboration becomes instinctive.

You'll know your team is working when its members truly believe that no one person can do a job alone. What actually builds a team is the sense of achievement people experience when they are a part of something bigger than any one individual.

5

Managing Conflict

Conflict is a normal part of the work process—so much so that managers typically spend 25 percent of each workday dealing with it. Under antagonistic conditions, it is not uncommon for that figure to rise to as high as 60 percent. Managers are frequently surveyed to determine their training and development needs. Typically, their responses suggest that conflict is a topic of growing importance. One survey, conducted some years ago by the American Management Association, rated conflict management "as a topic of equal or slightly higher importance than planning, communication, motivation, and decision making." The AMA findings also suggested that conflict-management ability would become increasingly important in years to come—a prediction that has certainly proved true.

Ever-increasing numbers of today's managers report feeling frustrated by their inability to settle workplace differences. Usually they work around conflict, truly believing resolution to be impossible. They have come to view the process of conflict resolution as fraught with disaster. They have found that it inevitably diverts energy, destroys morale, polarizes groups, and deepens differences—in other words, it results in a wide array of dysfunctional behaviors.

Many managers have extremely negative perceptions of conflict. Typically, these managers come from organizational backgrounds in which differing points of view were not allowed. They have an unchallenged belief that conflict is destructive and should therefore be avoided. As a result, they lack an appreciation for the creative aspects of blending different perspectives. They don't realize that a well-managed conflict-resolution process can uncover buried issues, open up new ideas, and inspire innovation. When there is a process to resolve it, conflict can provide a natural source of creativity, problem solving, and team building.

Sources of Conflict

So how do you develop a viable conflict-resolution process? You start by understanding the dynamics involved in organizational conflict. Many of these conflicts start small, but become magnified in an atmosphere of ambiguity, inconsistency, and uncertainty—an atmosphere prevalent within poorly run organizations that lack proper planning and decision-making processes. Most organizational conflicts can be traced to questions of authority and responsibility, competition for limited resources, lack of accountability, unclear work priorities, loosely enforced policies, lack of ethics and values, vague or unclear communications, and differing work-behavioral expectations.

The expectations that subordinates have for themselves are frequently different from those they have for their coworkers—and from those their coworkers have for them. When expectations differ, disagreements are inevitable. The varied ways in which people approach their jobs—how they obtain the desired results—also create conflict. Differing styles of work behavior can trigger what are perhaps the most common conflicts in the workplace—those that we refer to as "personality conflicts."

If subordinates are not provided with a management-supported mechanism for resolving their differences, they'll soon have difficulty working together. It doesn't take long for such disagreements to erode respect between people and between work units. So how do you get people with dissimilar behavior patterns to work together? The answer is to capitalize on the unique traits each behavioral style brings to the team. You can't just determine whose viewpoint should prevail. When the emphasis is placed on who's right and who's wrong, conflict becomes dysfunctionally competitive, or "you against me."

A landmark study conducted by Aamodt and Kimbrough at the University of Arkansas in 1981 demonstrated the importance of group composition for group dynamics. The researchers defined the purpose of the study as "to investigate the effects of group composition, based upon trait homogeneity-heterogeneity, on group problem-solving ability." Subjects were assigned to one of two groupings: One grouping was homogeneous, meaning that all members had similar traits, and the other grouping was heterogeneous, meaning that each person had dissimilar traits. Both groupings were given the same series of structured and unstructured tasks to resolve. Analysis of the results showed a significant difference in the quality of the decisions produced by the heterogeneous groupings.

The results and discussion section of the study stated, in part, "The results strongly suggest that group heterogeneity may lead to better group performance than that of groups composed of homogeneous individuals. This finding, especially if replicated with a larger number of groups and with different types of tasks, supports the notion of team building in organizations."

The Arkansas study concluded that groups of people with differing personalities performed better than groups in which everyone was the same. The underlying assumption in this study is that these heterogeneous groups were able to capitalize on their differences. In other words, they found a way to resolve conflict, or at least to keep conflict from blocking their ability to work together.

Many unfounded assumptions have been made regarding the value of working together in groups, one being that people will *always* perform better in a group than they will individually. Not so! This happens only when there is a means of resolving differences between the individuals in the group and between that group and other groups.

No-No List

Most people avoid openly discussing their most serious conflicts, wishing to avoid the negative consequences of disclosing their feelings. During our formative years, our parents and teachers, serving as social guides, warned us against the perils of outspokenness. Their teachings emphasized the value of cooperation and the importance of not making waves. Repetitive injunctions like, "If you can't say something nice, don't say anything at all," clearly warned us to keep our mouths closed in front of others—or at least to be careful what we said. The supposed intention of these childhood admonitions was to teach us not to offend people. It's more likely that the underlying (dysfunctional) purpose was to keep us from embarrassing our social guides in front of their peers.

Most of us can remember the condemnation that followed an innocent childhood disclosure of a family no-no in front of company. That lesson, once taught, is seldom forgotten. As adults, we still tend to avoid discussing issues that might provoke retribution. But as we form into groups, with our different styles, values, and behavior patterns, and try to work together, there are bound to be conflicts. Acting as though a conflict doesn't exist—treating it as a no-no—erects barriers within the group. If a work unit does not have a method for resolving conflict, that unit will eventually become dysfunctional.

This effect is cumulative: There is a direct correlation between the length of the no-no list and the level of dysfunction within a work unit. That is, the longer the list, the greater the dysfunction. It is important to understand how unresolved conflict, stored on the no-no list, relates to the development of organizational dysfunction. Let's review the formation of dysfunction, as detailed in Chapter 1. You'll remember it takes place in four stages:

1. *Ambiguity is not questioned.* For example, a vague directive has an employee being presented with two ways of doing something, but she does not point this out or ask for the conflict to be clarified.

2. *Inconsistencies are ignored.* For instance, a rule is followed by some people but broken by others, yet nothing happens to the rule violators.

3. *Ambiguities and inconsistencies are undiscussable.* It becomes politically incorrect to openly talk about the existence of ambiguities and inconsistencies. People won't risk getting themselves or others into trouble by sharing real issues and telling the truth.

4. *Undiscussability is undiscussable.* People ignore the fact that ambiguities and inconsistencies are never openly discussed. Silence during meetings not only implies that issues don't exist, but also signals that the absence of open discussion won't be talked about either.

You can tell when a no-no list exists because people will avoid open discussions of relevant issues. Rather, they bog down in never-ending debates over mundane issues like copy machine usage, personal telephone calls, office furniture, the computer system, and whether there should be macaroni or potato salad at the Christmas party.

Overreaction to a simple mistake is another clue that bigger, unstated conflicts are buried on the no-no list. The longer the list gets, the more tense and anxious people become and the more they avoid discussing conflicts for fear of a major blow-up. A long list also indicates the nonexistence of an effective conflict-resolution process. Few people can thrive for very long in the tension-filled environment that inevitably results from unresolved conflict.

Conflict Sequencing

Items are placed on the no-no list when they become a significant source of potential conflict. For example, two employees decide to air their differences in a good-faith attempt to resolve a conflict. Unfortunately, they get into an argument in which each "side" holds firm to its original position. The participants are discouraged. Instead of being resolved, their differences have been magnified. Disappointing experiences, especially when there has been an emotional investment, leave negative impressions. So regardless of how important it might be for this conflict to get resolved, it is not likely that these two folks will bring it up again—certainly not on their own. That issue goes on the no-no list. As time passes, other unit members will get into discussions of their differences and experience similar outcomes. The group's no-no list will lengthen, mistrust will set in, and a dysfunctional norm will become established. Unless the pattern changes, the list will continue to grow until the unit chokes on the volume of indigestible issues.

As a manager, you need to remember that your goal is not to *reduce* conflict but to *manage* conflict. Conflict is a natural source of creativity and the root element of synergy. Only when conflict is hidden or stored on the no-no list does it serve no useful purpose. Unresolved conflicts inhibit collective efforts by keeping people from exploring mutually supported alternatives. The goal of a conflict-resolution program is to bring conflict into a public forum where it can be properly examined and fully understood.

The purpose of conflict management is to work your way through the entire no-no list. Typically, the heaviest conflict issues top the list. Not only did they surface first, but they have been there so long that they have taken on additional weight. More recent items, which have been tacked onto the bottom of the list, are much less significant. You must start at the bottom with the least significant issues and work your way up the list. This is called *conflict sequencing.* Understanding how conflict sequencing works will help you to get to those deeper issues that are blocking teamwork.

According to Lois B. Hart in *Learning from Conflict: A Handbook for Trainers,* working through the conflict cycle (sequence) in this manner makes it "more likely the next conflict would be resolved more easily and with a higher level of satisfaction." The purpose of conflicting sequencing is to open up communication among participants and thus enable them to get to the deeper issues on the no-no list. If an issue cannot be resolved, then it is set aside so as not to block the conflict sequence. That issue may be revisited once progress has been made on other issues.

Let's examine the conflict sequence model, shown in Figure 5-1 and described below. (Note that this model is not designed to be used by the individuals in a group, but rather by a facilitator or manager in a group or team setting.) In the model, the arrows show movement through the sequence in a counterclockwise direction. That's to remind you that to resolve conflict, you must work backwards through time to discover the origin of the conflict. Unless you get to the root causes, nothing will happen to resolve the conflict. Instead, participants will simply keep track of how many points they can make by arguing with those who oppose them. The side with the most points wins when the other side gives up or stops arguing. The side that won will not bring the issue up again for fear that the opposition will have gathered the support of more powerful people, and the losing side won't bring it up again for fear of another defeat. The issue is not resolved, but simply added to the no-no list. This is known as the "zero-sum" game—the "winner" gets a plus (+) and the loser gets a minus (−), the sum of which is zero (0). If this game-playing continues, the work unit gains nothing and becomes dysfunctional because the participants cannot resolve their differences without keeping score.

The conflict sequence model has six stages:

1. *Tracking.* You begin tracking a conflict as soon as you suspect that one exists. Signs include raised eyebrows, caustic comments, unanswered requests, or overreactions to minor issues. Discussions focus on who was right or wrong. You notice employees closely watching management reactions.

Figure 5-1. The conflict sequence.

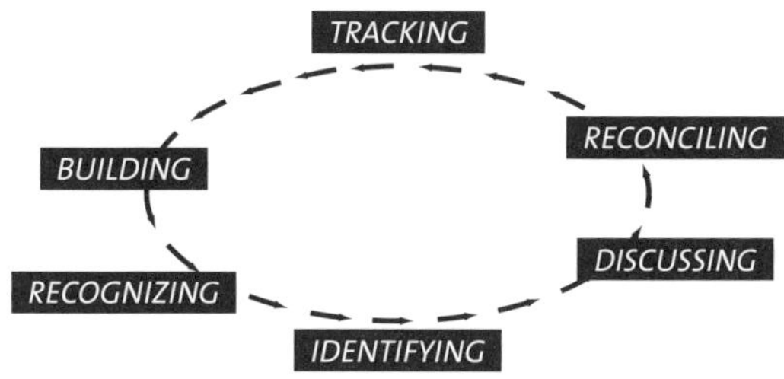

2. *Building.* You realize that rather than dissipating, the conflict is growing. The people involved will talk about the issues surrounding the conflict only in ambiguous terms, and continue to downplay misunderstandings. More people seem aware that the conflict exists, even if they don't fully understand who or what is involved. They are beginning to either choose sides or distance themselves to avoid involvement.

The next three stages of the conflict sequence are the core of the process. They outline the steps you, the manager, can take to get RID of the conflict and keep it from settling onto the no-no list. RID is an acronym standing for recognizing, identifying, and discussing. You begin to deal with conflict as you *recognize* that conflict exists, *identify* the source of it, and *discuss* a resolution. Let's examine each of those steps.

3. *Recognizing.* Conflict is apparent, and the issues need to be brought out into the open. Choose a strategy that acknowledges the conflict, while suspending judgment as to who or what is right or wrong.

- Make it clear what you're trying to accomplish.
- Share your objectives with key players and communicate your goals throughout the organization. (Your purpose must be legitimate—for example, to improve quality, decrease turnover, build morale, or increase productivity.)
- Select a disinterested third party to gather information from those directly involved.

4. *Identifying.* Pull the key players together to facilitate a nonjudgmental examination of the issues underlying the conflict. Explain that you are providing an opportunity for people who are known to be in conflict to communicate within the "security" of a group session. Encourage antagonists to share the basis for their views. Emphasize that you value individual contributions, but that you do want a joint resolution.

Blend expectations by focusing on the vantage points that

all participants have in the conflict. Ask them how it looks from where they sit. Encourage them to:

* Make a list of expectations for each person involved, together with their own expectations for getting the job done.
* Pinpoint the source of all unmet expectations.
* Identify the role of each player.
* Clarify the relative significance of each issue involved, and determine the priority of resolving them.
* Openly declare their willingness to continue the process until a resolution is agreed upon.

5. Discussing. Have the key players deliberate on the conflict. Explain resolution techniques and negotiation methods, and then have them state their expectations of the process.

Set the stage by documenting all attempts to resolve conflict.

* Openly examine what worked and what didn't.
* Don't downplay or cover up unsuccessful experiences; use them as opportunities to try again. Even if a resolution didn't occur, a major step was taken to get the conflict off the no-no list and out into the open. A basis for trust was established, thus making future conflict resolution less stressful for all parties.
* Encourage those who experienced minor success to continue to work through the process.
* Direct those with unresolved conflicts to focus on *what* needs to change rather than on *who* needs to change.

By this point, people should understand how the conflict has evolved and be ready to select a technique for resolution. Have them:

* Agree on a means of resolution.
* Appoint neutral monitors.

* Establish time lines and begin working on the resolution.

6. *Reconciling.* This is the last stage of the conflict sequence. It calls for reevaluation of the conflict, its underlying issues, and its resolution. Note the time lines established in the discussion process.

When appropriate, informally poll the key players and the neutral monitors and use the information they share with you to answer the following questions:

* Have the parties settled their differences?
* Are there any hurt feelings?
* Is any restitution necessary?
* Are participants meeting one another's expectations?
* What lessons have been learned?
* How should these lessons be applied to future conflict?

If further action is warranted, bring the involved parties together and revisit the above processes to address any unresolved aspects of the original conflict. Help them understand that resolution is vital, and that they are responsible for achieving it.

The Importance of Resolving Differences

In evaluating the need for conflict resolution, consider the fact that productivity is directly related to personal job satisfaction. As satisfaction drops, so does productivity. Personality conflicts, poor people interaction, and management temperament are among the primary causes of workplace friction. Without a conflict-resolution process, work-centered conflicts will damage relationships and drive people apart. Research shows that the most competent, functional workers will be the first to flee a hostile, dysfunctional workplace. Consider what it would mean should your best employees leave to seek harmony elsewhere.

Dysfunctional employees fear being wrong or worry that

their views are different. They see conflict as disagreement. To them, conflict is two-sided. They think, "If I'm right, then you must be wrong, but if the reverse is true, I don't want to know about it." A basic conflict-resolution program can be adapted to met the needs of any organization, work unit, or individual. Most of us are reluctant to listen to opposing views because we fear we will hear something that might weaken our position. In order to resolve conflict, this kind of thinking must be changed.

The ultimate goal of conflict management is to search for permanent solutions—deals don't last. Quick fixes need to be developed into long-lasting settlements. A closer look may reveal some of the deeper issues that are still festering. When given an opportunity to reflect on old conflicts, people often admit dissatisfaction with their hasty acceptance of a quick fix. Oftentimes, their first response was an evasive reaction. More discussion may be needed before a durable resolution is achieved. A productive resolution is often based on a blend of the participants' expectations. By taking the time to facilitate a permanent solution, you establish the basis for trust and commitment.

Training dysfunctional employees in conflict resolution places the responsibility for solving their problems on their shoulders, and frees up the manager for more profitable tasks. When a manager resolves a conflict between dysfunctional subordinates, the resolution belongs to the manager. The subordinates will continue to expect their manager to act as judge, which is time-consuming, unproductive, and potentially dysfunctional. Those being judged have nothing invested in the decision, so they don't feel responsible for either the problem or the means of ending it. More importantly, judgment fosters disagreement, disrespect, and disconnection.

Build a stronger sense of unity within your work team by avoiding the use of judgmental or disconnecting phrases such as:

Yeah, but . . .
I disagree.
You're wrong.

Everyone knows . . .
I may be wrong, but . . .
Correct me if I'm wrong.
What you don't understand is . . .

Such phrases set boundaries and discourage the further exploration of differing points of view, particularly from dysfunctional employees. Since the purpose of a conflict-management process is to collect as many views as possible, the goal is to draw participants into the process so that they feel connected.

The way to encourage connection, especially when there are strong people with divergent opinions, is to use phrases like:

Yes.
And . . .
Or . . .
Okay.
Good.
Thanks.

or any similar nonqualifying expression that shows that you have heard and appreciate what has been said. The use of connecting words makes the speaker feel that his or her contribution is recognized. Dysfunctional people are more likely to change their position and be more open to yours when they know that their current view has been acknowledged as valid and acceptable.

Managing conflict in a dysfunctional workplace involves selecting an appropriate resolution process, building a strategy that meets your needs, blending individual expectations, setting the stage for negotiation, and searching for permanent solutions. People who work together must learn how to express their concerns, ask difficult questions, and face the core issues that are keeping them from achieving success. Without an effective conflict-management process, no work unit can reach very high. Remember, if you don't manage conflict, conflict will manage you.

6

Visualizing Change

Nothing so quickly exposes individual or organizational dysfunction as *change.* It brings to the surface any number of dysfunctional behaviors that previously had been carefully concealed. These unforeseen factors sometimes prevent changes from happening as planned. Managers, looking for positive results, frequently are surprised by a downward shift in performance. When anticipated outcomes fail to materialize, dysfunctional employees are quick to point out that management should have left well enough alone. The refrains from these hard-core skeptics abound: "I don't see how changing things would have made any difference." "Any fool could have seen it wasn't going to work." "I've seen change come, and I've seen it go, and this too shall pass."

The major obstacle to implementing change is that few people can "see" it; they only sense it, and they don't like the way it feels—particularly the dysfunctional employees. When a change is first announced, it typically is described in mechanistic terms like profits, expenses, and sales. Performance expectations are measured by quotas, time lines, defects, delivery schedules, and benchmarks, factors that line staff rarely see and know little about. Suddenly, management makes a big deal out of changing a process that employees thought was working just fine, and shortly after the new system goes into effect, things go to pot and management gets upset at the workforce. What is most misunderstood about change is the impact it has on individual work behaviors, with negative human responses topping the list of reasons why employees resist.

Change is disruptive to the normal work flow and generates fear among dysfunctional employees. What they fear most is having their faults exposed. They're concerned that the introduction of new equipment or new ways of doing things may blow their cover and highlight their perceived incompetence. Functional employees see change as an opportunity to learn something new, to pick up additional skills, and to become a better person as a result.

This mismatch between functional and dysfunctional employees is what frequently brings change to a screeching halt. It can also generate unexpected and undesirable personnel issues. For example, a few years back, a medium-sized municipal government was in the middle of introducing quality circles throughout the organization when it ran into serious employee resistance. Department heads were reporting an unexpected rise in the number of dismissals, demotions, and disciplinary actions. An organizationwide survey, funded by the Federal Mediation and Conciliation Service, found that 80 percent of the behavioral problems were associated with the change in the way the organization was managed. Few of the 2,500 employees surveyed disagreed with the new participative style, but a significantly large number resisted it because, as one outspoken employee put it, "We couldn't see how quality circles would be any different from all the other stuff we've tried."

Obviously, there is more to implementing change than selecting an appropriate tactical strategy. Trust me: Your ability to overcome dysfunction in the workplace will be put to the test during any period of transition.

The Performance Pathway

Much has been written about the process of change and the importance of having a vision. It is clear from these readings that three critical questions need to be posed as the intended change is formulated: What is it that needs to change? What does it look like now? What will it look like after the changes? No matter how critical the change is, what really matters is that as it unfolds, it looks the same to everyone involved.

When those directly affected can see what the change means to them, they are more likely to support it. Your challenge is to show all your people what the change looks like, so that they can understand, appreciate, and accept what you have in mind.

The performance pathway model (Figure 6-1) brings the process into visual perspective by showing key factors that collectively influence job performance. The performance pathway begins with the individual, moves outward over a time line, and ends with a measurable outcome. It is designed as a visual aid to assist you in defining those factors that have a negative impact on a subordinate's performance during a period of change. The model is most helpful in isolating dysfunctional work behaviors.

Before we get started, take a moment and think of one or two employees whose work performance could use a booster shot right about now. Keep those folks firmly fixed in your

Figure 6-1. The performance pathway.

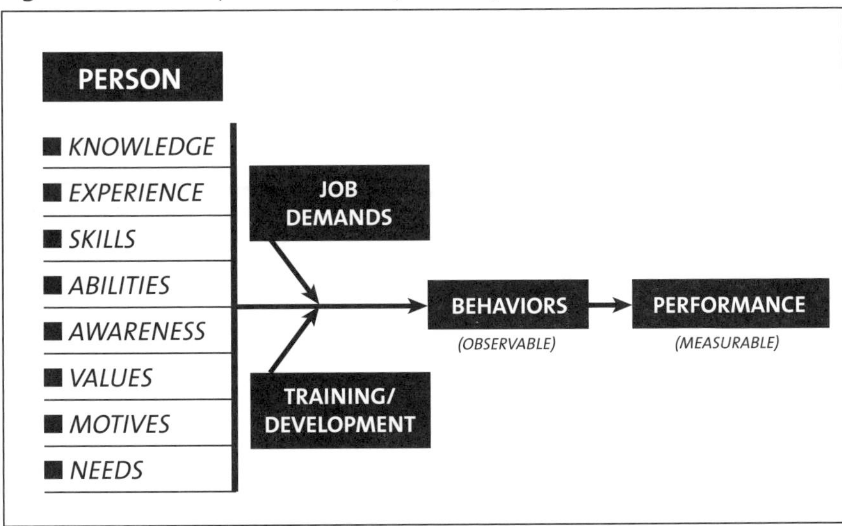

mind as you learn how to apply the Pathway model in your workplace.

Person

Individuals bring many traits and characteristics with them to the job. Some are desirable (functional), while others are undesirable (dysfunctional). Figure 6-1 identifies eight factors that can affect on-the-job performance. As individuals grow accustomed to the job, these essential factors undergo change.

For functional employees, these factors change in positive ways. For example, their *knowledge* increases, their *experience* broadens, their *skills* develop, their *abilities* improve, their *awareness* grows, their *motives* strengthen, their *needs* expand, and their *values* deepen. Such people are ready for change and will easily adjust to whatever comes their way.

Dysfunctional people bring these same traits to the job, but unlike their functional counterparts, they're looking for the status quo rather than improvement. Typically, it takes them longer to get accustomed to the job. Meanwhile, they're searching for the minimum acceptable requirements and not thinking about performance. The last thing they want to see is change.

Job Demands

These are the conditions under which the person is expected to perform the job. Unlike a job description, which lists tasks and duties, job demands define work in terms of past, present, and future expectations. For example, was the person hired or promoted because of past job performance, present job requirements, or future job potential? Functional employees relish the opportunity for advancement and greater responsibility, while dysfunctional persons in the same job are threatened by an increase in job demands. Dysfunctional employees are content with jobs that never change, while functional employees get bored without opportunities for growth and development.

Training/Development

Training relates to short-term upgrades and improvements. Development has an evolutionary focus related to future growth and potential. The maintenance of individual skill levels is determined by the organization's training and development philosophy. For example, if the philosophy is to hire or promote people who are fully trained and ready to perform, emphasis must be placed on the recruitment and selection processes. Higher levels of performance are expected in a shorter period of time. On the other hand, if people are trained and developed on the job, the organization will need experienced trainers and skilled evaluators. Performance expectations are lower, and people are given more time to get it right.

Behaviors

The actions people take in response to their work environment are observable. People react to conditions in functional and dysfunctional ways. Job-related behaviors, if observed carefully, can provide the manager with the first clue that people are accepting or rejecting change. For example, functional people can be seen moving forward, trying new things, and making change happen, while dysfunctional individuals are holding back, avoiding anything new, and reverting to the old ways.

Performance

Performance is the measurable outcome of the interactions among the person, job demands, training/development, and behaviors. Here, at the end of the pathway, is where you discover what worked and what didn't. The results of all your plans are reflected at this final stage. But this is also a beginning—a place to start again. Armed with the results, you are now in a position to show the functional people how to retrace their steps and target specific areas for improvement. The dysfunctional folks can benefit by walking through the model step by step while you point out where, what, and how they can do better next time.

Strategic Application

According to the pathway model, performance is sustained by maintaining a balance between job demands and training/development. This means that training/development is provided in anticipation of future job changes. New elements are introduced to the job only when employees demonstrate confidence in their skills and abilities. It makes no sense for you to wait until performance declines before you provide training. Don't forget that dysfunctional employees are reluctant to admit that they don't know how to do something. That means that it will be up to you to disclose their weak spots and keep their job skills current.

In the pathway model, long-term growth is achieved by assessing future job demands and providing developmental opportunities for people beyond their current capabilities. Keeping track of employees' performance is important, but knowing their *potential* is critical. Matching their future expectations with your future needs is what improves performance and sustains growth.

As time passes and job demands change, employees accept that at some point in the future, things will need to be done differently. However, if their forthcoming duties and responsibilities are beyond their knowledge, skills, and abilities, they will be affected negatively, and the performance pathway will be driven downward, resulting in a performance loss.

In this dysfunctional situation, management takes action after the fact, belatedly providing training to those persons most negatively affected by the change. Rather than remedying a bad situation, this training may simply escalate the tension. Why? Unless the purpose of the training is made clear, a major clash in expectations is bound to occur between the manager and the employee. The manager will expect performance to improve, while the employee is expecting to achieve equilibrium—to return to the prechange level of performance. If performance does not improve after the training, the manager decries the waste of time and money, and the employee gets a poor performance evaluation. It's no wonder change brings about fear in people.

There is wisdom in the saying, "The certainty of misery is better than the misery of uncertainty." People would prefer to know in advance how change will affect them—the bad as well as the good. In a functional scenario, people are prepared for the change before it occurs. If you want positive acceptance of change, you should hold frequent meetings; publish charts, graphs, or plans; and share your view of what is about to happen. It is up to you to create a vision of what the future looks like in the minds of those most affected by the change. Training people to prepare for change will affect their behavior positively and drive the pathway upward, resulting in a performance gain.

Change affects the performance pathway when it affects any of the five factors identified in the model. The most likely impact point(s) vary from one type of organization to another. For example, change usually enters the service-oriented organization in the form of new or additional customer requests, concerns, and expectations (job demands). In technology-driven enterprises, change frequently takes the form of requests for state-of-the-art equipment, system upgrades, and additional staff (training/development).

Educational institutions, for the most part, ignore change until the public, through the political system, legislates major reform. In response, administrators hire consultants to conduct studies that prove that reform isn't necessary, claiming instead that they need more classrooms, more equipment, and more money. The performance pathway functions most affected here are job demands and performance, meaning (unfortunately) higher expectations for teachers.

Government agencies are more used to change than any other sector, since their operations and procedures are defined by legislation and therefore are constantly changing. The problem is, those changes usually arise from political decisions that could be overturned after the next election. Low performance expectations and high levels of ambiguity and inconsistency attract dysfunctional employees. So, the most likely performance pathway factors to be influenced here are training/development and behaviors.

Health-care providers either ignore change or get caught

up in the ambiguity of competing demands for patient services and medical technology. The introduction of managed care has forced health-care providers to change the way they think about economics and competition. The performance pathway factors most affected by the changes in health care are performance and behavior. Expectations of higher performance are flushing out many dysfunctional employees who historically made a comfortable home for themselves in health care.

Knowing the factors in your organization that are most likely to be affected can help you respond to change in a proactive rather than a reactive manner.

How People React to Change

Generally, people react to change in three different ways. Some are proactive/assertive. They view change as a way of making improvements within the organization. Others are reactive/aggressive, and respond to change by trying to stop it. The remaining group consists of people who are inactive/submissive; they won't take a stand one way or the other. The level of dysfunction that exists in an organization is determined by the size and influence of the latter two groups. To wit:

* *Proactive/assertive* people are progressive in their approach to change. They tend to value innovation and respond positively to negative comments, difficult challenges, collective concerns, and personal criticisms. Their most notable characteristics are anticipating change, making things happen, problem solving, and self-assessment.

* *Reactive/aggressive* people are negative about most things and tend to openly resist change in counterproductive ways. Their survival instinct is strong, and they are quick to feel threatened. These individuals avoid responsibility and, when things go wrong, shift the blame to someone else. Their most notable characteristics are finger-pointing, outright resistance, overt obstruction, and sabotage.

⋆ *Inactive/submissive* people are neutral toward growth and development, and go along with change without enthusiasm. They avoid offending others by sidestepping commitments and dodging serious issues. They accept change only when they see it working. Their most notable characteristics are fence-sitting, limited approval, qualified support, and conditional agreements.

In order to overcome dysfunction in your workplace, you must learn to recognize dysfunctional behaviors and understand the impact they are having. Start by assessing the current level of dysfunction. Then you will be able to develop a set of management practices that have a three-pronged purpose: (1) to reinforce functional behaviors, (2) to discontinue dysfunctional practices, and (3) to help those in the middle make the right choices.

Controlling Rumors

Management most frequently gets blamed for failing to provide adequate, timely, helpful, and accurate information about the status of change. However, when challenged, dysfunctional employees confess that despite all the meetings they attend, all the memos they get, and all the direction they are given, they still rely a great deal on the informal information they get from rumors.

Now, it is human nature to gossip and speculate about the people and events around us. And it is understandable that we are curious about one another, and about how impending change might affect our welfare. During periods of change, everyone's strengths, weaknesses, hot buttons, and problems quickly become grist for the rumor mill.

Being in on things is an important motivator for dysfunctional employees. Passing rumors helps them to feel important and useful. So it is natural that change would generate fear among dysfunctional employees. In the minds of dysfunctional employees, any form of organizational change means shifting from familiar ways to ways they didn't ask for and don't understand. No matter how positive a spin management tries to put on it, transition is scary because it raises the level of ambiguity, inconsistency, and uncertainty, all of which add to the flow of misinformation and rumors. The fear of personal loss forms the basis of most rumors during periods of transition.

One way to quell rumors is to address the individual fears generated by the transition. Your credibility will be enhanced if you listen to and acknowledge what people are trying to say. Be alert to simple expressions that voice serious concerns. The following samples are listed under the category that best fits the loss being described.

- *Loss of identity,* expressed by such questions as:
  Who am I?
  What's wrong with me?
  Why do I need to change?
- *Loss of control,* captured in such queries as:
  I didn't ask for this—whose idea was this?
  Doesn't anyone care about me?
  What will they do to me next?
- *Loss of meaning,* characterized by such questions as:
  Why is this happening to me?
  Why was I singled out?
  I've been here for fifteen years; doesn't that count?
- *Loss of belonging,* identified by queries like:
  Does this mean I'll be moved?
  Who will I be working with?
  Why can't I be with people I know?
- *Loss of future,* as employees ask:
  Doesn't my hard work count anymore?
  Do I have to start over?
  How am I supposed to get promoted now?

You can't simply ignore rumors. When rumors get out of control, dysfunctional employees have difficulty coping with both personal and organizational problems. Functional employees don't respond to rumors until they fully understand what is being disclosed. Dysfunctional employees who get caught up in feeding the rumor mill are eventually discredited by their functional coworkers, once the actual facts become known. Even if those facts soothe the original anxieties, you are left with an erosion of trust and respect between you and your employees.

It is up to management to minimize the negative effect of rumors by creating a stronger information feedback loop. Try following these simple guidelines:

* *Provide official clarification on any and all rumors.* Ignoring a rumor is the worst thing you can do. Be open with employees. Unless you are bound by some legal restriction, when you hear a rumor, regardless of the content, tell everyone everything you know about the facts of the matter. Don't wait until you have all the details—just get the truth out there, fast. If some of what you say turns out to be inaccurate, then retell it the right way as soon as you get a chance. You may have to do this several times.
* *Seek out reliable sources of information among employees.* Accurate information travels best with those you know to be reliable. Find out who is trustworthy among the staff and talk to those people yourself. Tell them that you want to know the truth about what is really happening. Ask them not to embellish on what they tell you. Let them know that if you find out that they can't be trusted, you won't rely on them again. Everyone wants to be trusted with the truth.
* *Pass along what you know in a neutral manner.* This may sound harsh, but employees don't care what you think, nor do they want your opinion. They only want to know what you know. Keep your attitude and feelings to yourself. Avoid comments about the wisdom of change, or the likelihood that it will or won't work. Report only the facts that you know firsthand. If employees have opinions to share with you, acknowledge them without comment.

Transition Monitoring

When people lose sight of who they are during a transition, they won't give much thought to who you need them to be.

Dysfunctional employees need to believe that they have some degree of control over their work life. Even though people may not actually lose their jobs, they are afraid that they might, and they often react on this basis. It's hard for people to accept change unless they feel good about it. Organizational efforts to motivate people are easily discounted when dysfunctional employees perceive a threat to their work-group dynamics.

Comments from dysfunctional employees often take on a depressing tone. These employees feel disconnected from the past and don't care much about the future. While you're trying to move the organization ahead by doing things differently, the dysfunctional employees want everything back the way it used to be.

Consultant-author William Bridges is widely acclaimed as an authority on organizations in transition. In his book *Managing Transitions: Making the Most of Change,* Bridges states that management is responsible for creating an environment of organizationwide readiness for change. The following list of developmental activities is taken primarily from his book, with some added features that are specifically geared toward helping dysfunctional employees get through a transition.* The challenge is to work as many of these activities as you can into your operational systems and procedures:

1. Define the terms of the transition and the changes that are likely to occur.
2. Identify individuals and groups that will be the most severely affected by the changes.
3. Monitor the readiness of each work unit as measured by its communication systems, structural flexibility, cultural dynamism, and morale:
   - How are the changes being perceived?
   - How well are the changes understood and accepted?

*William Bridges, *Managing Transitions: Making the Most of Change* (Reading, Mass.: Addison Wesley Longman, 1991), p. 42. © Copyright 1991 by William Bridges and Associates, Inc. Reprinted by permission of Addison Wesley Longman.

- What is each work unit's openness to these changes?
- How broad is the support for these changes?
- How much does it polarize the workforce?
- Are the current behaviors and attitudes of the leadership consonant with the changes being envisioned?

4. Analyze the political implications of these changes.
5. Set a challenging pace for each phase of the change.
6. Form a transition monitoring team to keep track of what is happening to people during the cultural change.
7. Identify the new skills and knowledge required by these changes and find or develop internal training and educational programs for those affected.
8. Provide coaching for dysfunctional employees to help them change.
9. Conduct interventions in those work units most resistive to change.
10. Review the communication within each work unit and make adjustments as necessary to keep people informed.

Transition Monitoring Team

Bridges strongly recommends item 6, above—the formation of a transition monitoring team. This team consists of seven to twelve key people who represent a cross section of the organization. Key people are those folks whom you want on your side during the transition. Without their energy and support, the change will never get off the ground, let alone fly. They should be well respected throughout the organization—people whose coworkers are known to seek their advice and to look to them for leadership when the going gets tough.

You may also want to invite one or two of the known "troublemakers" to be part of this monitoring team. Troublemakers are those who don't go along just to get along. They pose the hard questions and challenge every directive that comes from management. Do not confuse troublemakers with dysfunctional employees. They are not "in trouble" because they don't work hard—quite the contrary. It is because they are so good at what they do that they have time to stir things up, and management has trouble dealing with them. These folks are also described as "difficult to handle."

The transition monitoring team (TMT) meets with a facilitator every week or two to take the pulse of the organization as it moves through the process of change. The monitoring team has no decision-making power and is not empowered to take any action. Its purpose, according to Bridges, is to facilitate upward communication and to do three other things:

1. The TMT demonstrates that management wants to know how things are going for people.
2. The TMT is an effective focus group to review plans or communications before they are announced.
3. The TMT provides a point of ready access to the organization's grapevine and so can be used to correct misinformation and counter negative rumors.

The Importance of Sharing Information

Effective management in a fast-paced climate requires a high degree of information sharing. As the term implies, information sharing is a two-way process—a combination of what is disclosed to employees and the feedback received from them.

Sharing information with your top performers is especially important. Contrary to what you might expect, high achievers are not threatened by change itself—in fact, they often thrive during periods of change. They do, however, need to know a lot about the change if they are to stay with the organization. Successful people are constantly networking and are usually aware of better opportunities elsewhere. If you look as if you're not clear about how the change will be managed, the top performers may leave. Your best people need to know that they have opportunities for personal growth and professional development. They also need to know how to reach higher performance levels.

This point can't be stressed enough: Sharing information is a key factor in keeping good people. During periods of change, information sharing can be the most powerful tool a manager possesses. Keeping people informed increases their self-esteem. Consequently, they are more likely to be creative, offer ideas and suggestions, speak frankly, and get more involved by bringing unexplored problems to light.

Today's successful organization desperately needs managers who can communicate in a manner that encourages dysfunctional employees to become self-directed, self-accountable, and independent problem solvers who can think for themselves. When dysfunctional employees trust in the information-sharing process, they are more likely to believe that they are important to the organization, that management is the best source for accurate communication, and that what you say matters.

The Light at the End of the Tunnel

Toward the end of a recent seminar on managing change, someone passed out a phony announcement that read, "Attention: Due to budget cuts, the light at the end of the tunnel is being turned off." While it got a big laugh, it wasn't far from the truth. Change is like a tunnel—it's long, dark, narrow, and scary. Seeing the light keeps people moving, especially if they're following somebody who can show them the way. If the light is turned off, or if they can't see it from their position, they are less willing to enter the tunnel.

People take in information in three ways: They see it, hear it, or feel it. Research by neurolinguists has concluded that about 60 percent of us are visual processors—we believe or act on what we can see. Even those who use the other modalities (touch, hearing, etc.) will form an image in their mind of what they hear or feel. Whoever said, "A picture is worth a thousand words," must have understood this process very well. The challenge of change, then, is to create a community vision so that everyone can "see" what you mean and picture his or her role in the scene. That vision should shine like a beacon at the end of the tunnel.

7

Raising Expectations

Have you ever found yourself in a situation in which your expectations were not met? You could probably name quite a few. For the sake of discussion, consider the following hypothetical story:

Say you just signed up for a training seminar. What are your expectations? What has motivated you to go? What has to happen to make the session worthwhile?

Fast forward a little. Now the seminar is finished. Have your expectations been met? If so, you are satisfied and consider the fee to be money well spent. If not, you may experience what psychologists call an "ego bruise." That is, you could end up berating yourself with "should haves," as in, "I should have known better. I should have checked this out. I should have stayed at home."

Those "should" messages keep coming until you realize that *this is not your fault.* The "should" shifts to where it belongs: with the seminar presenter. *He* should have been prepared. *He* should have given you more for the money. *He* should refund your money. And so on, until all the "shoulds" are out. Unless the seminar sponsors do something quickly to change your mind, your feelings of disappointment and dissatisfaction will be permanently linked to their products. Most likely, you will disassociate or disconnect yourself so that the negative experience you had will never be repeated.

You may never share your feelings with the seminar sponsors. So, they will never get a chance to offer you a better response and perhaps shift your feelings about their seminars from the "Dis-List" to the "In-List" (as you will see in Figure 7-2). Don't let that happen with your employees. If their unmet expectations are not addressed in a proactive manner, *they* are liable to disassociate or disconnect themselves from *you.*

An expectation is always followed by a response, whether that response is positive, negative, or neutral. (Even *no* response is a response.) The connection or distance between an expectation and a response is measured by a time line. This time factor can encompass the few seconds it takes to answer the telephone, the weeks spent looking for a job, or the years involved in raising children.

Fictitious Frontiers

If our expectations are high and we are looking forward to a positive response, we want the time line between now and then to be shorter. Remember how, as a child, you counted the days until Christmas, birthdays, school vacation, etc.? We still look forward to weekends, holidays, and vacations. But what if our expectations are low because the response might be negative or unpleasant? A functional person would try to prepare for the consequences and hope to get them over with as soon as possible. A dysfunctional person, on the other hand, would want to extend the time line to avoid or postpone the consequences for as long as possible.

In the workplace, getting management to lower its expectations is one method that dysfunctional employees use to avoid potentially negative outcomes. This often happens when management states expectations that dysfunctional employees fear will be difficult to meet. If that strategy doesn't work, they might next attempt to extend the time line, hoping that management will either change its mind or forget the original objective entirely. Repeatedly putting things off is a characteristic of a dysfunctional employee. That is not to say that delaying an outcome is always dysfunctional. There are frequently worthy reasons to extend a time line or drop it altogether (more on this in Chapter 8). Perhaps the additional time truly would result in a better or more improved response. But if the reason for the delay is suspect, you may be dealing with a *fictitious frontier.*

Fictitious frontiers are illusive barriers that dysfunctional employees construct when they want to put off doing something or to avoid dealing with undesirable or unexpected consequences. New challenges can be scary and threatening to dysfunctional employees. When they aren't sure what you expect or fear that they can't come up with what is needed on time, they create a diversion that postpones their response. By extending their response time, they hope to lower or eliminate management's future expectations.

One example of a fictitious frontier is the "September syndrome." It normally starts about May or June, depending on when school lets out. When you assign a new project, employees respond by suggesting that "We should wait until September when the kids are back in school," or "Maybe we should wait until September, when everyone is back from vacation."

"After the new year" is another example. You begin to hear that phrase in October starting with the back-to-back federal holidays. It picks up momentum at Thanksgiving as the shopping season kicks into high gear. When you ask for a quick turnaround on a job, you get responses like, "Everyone will be busy with the holidays coming up. Why don't I wait until after the new year?" Or, "It's too late to finish this before the holidays. I'll start on it after the new year."

Years ago, when the economy was agriculturally based, kids got out of school for the summer to help tend the fields. It made sense to postpone nonfarm work until after the September harvest. Once the fields were reaped and the grain stored away, it was time to prepare for the traditional family feasts and celebrations. The frozen ground couldn't be worked until spring, so families gathered around the kitchen at

Thanksgiving and filled up on grandma's goodies through Christmas and on into the new year.

Given the tremendous changes that have affected the traditional family organization—i.e., the high divorce rates, the rise in single-parent families, and the breakup of the extended family, coupled with a growing service economy and high unemployment—maybe it is time to question these family/organization traditions and separate reality from fiction.

The Expectations Model

It is common practice for dysfunctional employees to keep a list of fictitious frontiers handy in case they feel uncomfortable about meeting your expectations or response times. One way to separate a fictitious frontier from a real time impediment is to work through the following expectations model with the affected employees. Don't be afraid to challenge whatever fictitious frontiers you come across. Traditional events such as holidays, vacations, or celebrations; promotional searches; personnel vacancies; equipment purchases; system upgrades; takeovers, reorganizations, buyouts, and mergers; and management programs are all likely candidates.

Matching expectations is neither an art nor a science. It is more like a process—one that unfolds in interconnected stages. The time line from the start of the process (the expectation) to the finish (the response) is always going to be affected by situations, behaviors, and feelings. Sometimes very little of this process can be controlled. But an understanding of each aspect of it can be used, in turn, to help everyone involved to better understand (and in some cases change) either the expectation or the response, or both.

Let's examine the five stages in the expectations model more closely (see Figure 7-1).

Expectation

Something is desired or anticipated, which in turn leads to additional expectations from each person involved. The ob-

Figure 7-1. Expectations model.

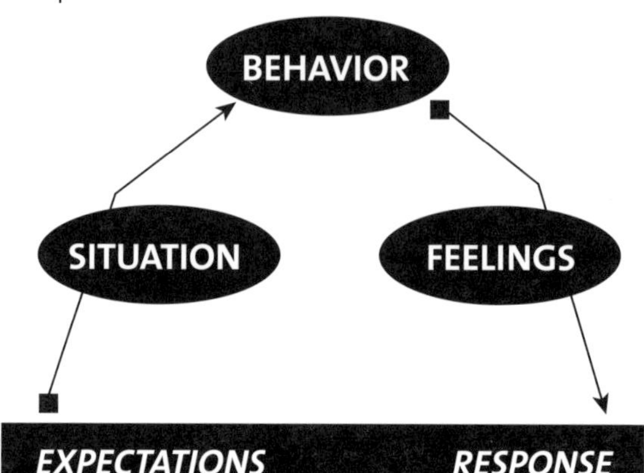

jective is to consider all possible viewpoints. You know what you, as manager, want to have happen. Ask yourself this: "What do the employees see from where they sit? What do they expect to happen? What do they expect from me?" Providing satisfaction is predictive. If you're willing to look, you can "see" what employees expect.

Situation

When dysfunctional employees get what they expect, they are pleased with themselves. If a situation arises that changes the outcome, you can count on them to hold someone else accountable. Your objective is to help the dysfunctional employee understand how the situation has affected the outcome. The trick is to control those situations that are likely to prevent employees from having their expectations met.

Behavior

Most expectations are based on myopic self-interest. This means that dysfunctional employees expect you to know what they need and to provide it. If your response matches their expectations, they behave positively. If it doesn't, they complain that you should have given them what they wanted, or that you should have tried harder to please them. In other words, they "should" on you.

Feelings

The feelings shown on the expectations model can be broken into two distinct categories, the "Dis-List" and the "In-List," as shown in Figure 7-2. Note the summary term at the bottom of each list.

As you can well imagine, people are much happier working from the In-List. That fact was brought home to me recently when I had an opportunity to observe teamwork among different surgery teams in a hospital. I noticed that the nurses gathered around the bulletin board each morning as the daily surgery schedule was posted. In addition to looking for room assignments, they were checking to see which surgeon had been assigned to their team. I overheard the nurses commenting on which doctors they liked and which they didn't. They were very matter-of-fact about it: "I like him, and I don't like her." I thought at first that these selections were based on personality or gender, but this was not the case. When asked, the nurses said that they liked those doctors who made their expectations known. Keeping the nurses informed created a sense of inclusion within the operation room. Thus involved,

Figure 7-2. Feelings: Dis-List vs. In-List.

Dis-List	*In-List*
Disrespected	Involved
Disappointed	Instrumental
Distrusted	Interested
Disconnected	Included
Disillusioned	Industrious
Discouraged	Informed
Disorderly	Integrity
Disruptive	Integral
Disintegration	Inquisitive
Discontinuity	Instinctive
DISEASED	INSPIRED

the nurses could anticipate the needs of the surgeon and respond appropriately.

When similarly questioned, the surgeons who were "liked" also shared their likes and dislikes of certain nurses, and for much of the same reasons. When the nurses and surgeons kept each other informed, the team was inspired to work in harmony. As a team they prepared for each operation with high expectations for themselves and, more importantly, for their patients.

When expectations are met, dysfunctional employees are left with good feelings—those on the In-List. Unmet expectations typically leave them feeling disappointed, discouraged, or disillusioned. Dysfunctional employees will hold you responsible for their negative feelings. They are not likely to share their most potent feelings. They would rather walk away and say nothing to you, to avoid the potentially negative consequences of disclosure. Your challenge is to enable them to safely express their negative feelings without putting them through an uncomfortable or embarrassing process.

Response

As a manager, one of your primary goals is to match your response to your employees' expectations. Your secondary goal is to respond proactively to those situations in which unmet expectations have developed. Your final goal is to rectify unmet expectations or get your dysfunctional employees to accept an alternative response.

Obviously, the response arrived at through the expectations model can be either positive or negative. When the response is positive—your expectations have been met and you've gotten the response you wanted—there is seldom cause for reflection. You simply pronounce yourself wise and wonderful. In the context of management, you have correctly guessed what your subordinates expected of you and therefore are a good manager. The outcome is easily understood and needs no further explanation—*unless you don't know why it happened and therefore don't know how to bring it about again.*

Valuative Coaching

Clearly, one goal of any organization should be to satisfy its functional employees by overcoming the dysfunction in their workplace. Yet many managers struggle with this concept. Finding ways to raise the expectations of dysfunctional employees is not as easy as one might think. Start by listing what you think they might possibly expect from you. Then focus on their vantage points as you review what you expect of them.

Consider how your responses look from where they stand. Identify any potential source of unmatched expectations. In other words, which of your expectations are higher than theirs? (It is not likely to be the other way around.)

Next, provide opportunities for employees you feel are dysfunctional to communicate within the relative security of an impartial focus group or confidential interview session. Only by collecting their points of view will you get the whole picture. Don't be discouraged if they are hesitant to respond at first. Once you have done this a few times, the dysfunctional employees will begin to understand what you want from them. Eventually, you will produce a set of mutually inclusive management-employee expectations.

Differing work-behavioral expectations are a major source of dysfunction in the workplace. Dysfunctional employees will need to find a way to share their individual expectations with you directly. By focusing on the vantage points of dysfunctional employees, you may pinpoint the source of your unmet expectations. And with some *valuative coaching*, you may get them to raise their sights a little.

Valuative coaching is simply providing dysfunctional employees with an understanding of where they stand, an awareness of how they are doing, and a perspective of what they need to change.

An account of my own experience may best illustrate the nature of valuative coaching.

When I was playing right tackle for my high school football team, a particular option play required me to lead the blocking for the running back. The play never seemed to work, since most of the time the defense had already smothered the running back before I could set my block.

During practice one day, our coach noticed that each time that play was called, I was telegraphing it by setting up with my right foot further back. Instead of yelling at me, he asked me to figure out a way to make the play work. I finally decided that if I lined up with my right foot set back on *every* play, I would not tip off the play.

The next game, when that play was called, my block took out the linebacker, and the running back was sprung free for a long gain. Later, when the coach praised the back for a good run, he, in turn, said that it was my block that had made it possible. The coach was very pleased, and I knew why.

Productive resolution must be based on a blend of expectations. The challenge is to find a way of coaching dysfunctional employees that will lead them to higher expectations and more satisfying responses. Valuative coaching is a way to reach dysfunctional employees in a nonthreatening manner.

As you begin the coaching process, it might be wise to walk the dysfunctional employee through the expectations model so that he or she fully understands your expectations. Have a list of those responses that met your expectations as well as those that didn't. Using the model, first discuss the employee's expectations in those instances in which he or she responded appropriately. Emphasize that what the employee did is valued and encourage him or her to do more. Then go over those situations in which the response did not match your expectations. As in my football story, try to determine what happened from the employee's point of view. Take this opportunity to make him or her aware of what needs to be done differently. Finally, provide a summary of your expectations for the future.

For example, let's say that you are interested in promoting teamwork, so you expect employees to:

- Do what they do best as often as they can.
- Share what they know.
- Point out mistakes.
- Work together to solve problems.
- Focus energy toward a common purpose.

* Promote a positive image of the team.
* Sustain good working relationships.
* Encourage mutual exploration of conflict.
* Develop skills through self-education.
* Build an atmosphere of mutual trust.

Changing Responses

Workplace expectations stem from a lifelong exposure to societal injunctions and homilies, such as, "Don't make promises you can't keep," and "Honesty is the best policy." Sure, some of us are cynical at times. But for the most part, we grow up expecting everyone to know right from wrong and to do the right thing. Speaking generally, the working public believes it has the right to expect fair and equal treatment.

Slowly, but inevitably, functional employees are getting harder to find. Their expectations are becoming a driving force in the marketplace.

Today, attracting good employees and keeping them is a challenge. The trend toward employee satisfaction is already affecting the private, for-profit world and is rapidly moving into the not-for-profit sector. The swelling momentum behind reinventing, reshaping, and reengineering is forcing all organizations to become more "employee-friendly."

As functional employees gain confidence in their power to influence results, their expectations will rise even further. Successful managers must find ways to match organizational responses with the expectations of functional employees, or risk losing them. In our fast-paced, high-demand, competition-driven workplace, don't expect functional employees to give you a second opportunity to address their problems. They don't have to. Assuming the economy continues to be strong, functional employees will have more choices. If you can't meet their expectations, they'll find someone who will. And who does that leave you with?

Your challenge is to keep the functional high achievers satisfied long enough to raise the expectations of the dysfunctional employees. Once you understand the dynamics in play in the expectations model, you should be in a better position to do both.

8

Looking Ahead

The part of my consulting assignments that I enjoy most is meeting with groups of hourly workers. It is from them that I learn what is really happening inside their organization. One way I get them to open up is to pose a series of questions, which they are to answer by raising their hands. First, I ask, "How many of you do not need a boss to tell you how to do your job?" Most of their hands go up. This is quickly followed by, "How many did not raise your hand because you were afraid your boss would find out?" More hands go up. Then I say, "Based on the show of hands, I conclude that you don't need a boss! Is that correct?" A resounding "No!" quickly follows. I then profess not to understand what they mean, and pose a final question: "Well, if you don't need a boss to tell you what to do, then why do you need a boss?" Their answer is always, "To give us direction."

Seafarers understand the perils of getting under way without a proper set of charts. If the navigator doesn't know what heading to maintain, then the ship sails at the mercy of the changing winds. It can easily be blown off course, with disastrous consequences. Yet how often have you seen top management desperately scrambling to keep the "ship" from running aground? Such reactionary efforts are a major source of dysfunction in the workplace.

You may be one of those middle managers who's struggling to stay afloat because of misdirection by senior executives who don't look ahead, focusing instead on bottom-line results and quick fixes. If that sounds familiar, stay tuned; this chapter will provide some welcome relief and some helpful suggestions.

In a dysfunctional organization, planning is a bothersome task, one that is neither understood nor appreciated. If a plan exists, you can bet that it was hastily developed at last year's management retreat. If you'd like to read it, you'll probably find it on an obscure shelf in a plastic binder, gathering dust alongside plans from previous years. One by one, each died a quiet death, drowned in a sea of unforeseen events.

Does this mean that if top management fails to provide direction, your crew cannot survive the turbulent waters ahead? Of course not. Like your seagoing counterparts, you yourself must continue to move ahead and keep pace with the prevailing winds. To keep your crew on course, you must show them how to respond faster, reduce costs, improve efficiency, and adjust to change. If those charged with planning and directing your organization are dysfunctional, then it may be up to you and others at your level to find a way to get ahead on your own.

Shifting Focus

In preceding chapters the focus has been on dysfunction in those around you and below you. It's time to shift the focus to those who influence you from above. If you accept that there have always been dysfunctional people in organizations, it stands to reason that some of them will have "floated" to the top. Despite the lack of attention paid to dysfunction in management literature, there have always been dysfunctional people in our organizations, at all levels—from the highest levels of senior management to the lowliest subordinate. The combination of their individual level of dysfunction and their level of power within the organization determines the impact their behavior may have upon the organization—and the impact you can have upon their behavior.

Coping with a dysfunctional boss is far more difficult than working with a dysfunctional subordinate. The impact of each on the organization is also very different. Dysfunction at the subordinate level affects production, customer service, quality, materials, waste, turnover, safety, absenteeism, etc. These are all performance-based characteristics that are measurable and easily changed, once you decide to do so.

Dysfunction at the top takes more sinister forms, such as favoritism, racism, sexism, nepotism, cronyism, and ageism. These organizational characteristics affect values and culture. They defy measurement and are difficult for you to change—especially from below.

At the higher levels, dysfunction is less about performance and more about power. Functional executives use their power to move things along, to overcome obstacles and resistance to changes, and to get the job done right. They focus on organizational performance through personal achievement. In contrast, dysfunctional executives use their power to keep things from happening while they figure out how to take the credit should something work and how to avoid responsibility should it fail. Putting previously agreed-upon actions on hold is a telltale sign of a dysfunctional decision maker. Overriding the recommendations of subordinates and making arbitrary decisions with no explanation are additional signs of a dysfunctional boss.

The life of an organization, its principles, ethics, style, values, and morality, are shaped by the actions of those at the top. Executives who hire their friends and relatives, overlook minorities, promote incompetent subordinates, and contract with suppliers who return favors are shaping a dysfunctional culture. Yet it would be difficult to get them to admit that such actions are demoralizing.

You may be wondering how such dysfunctional managers reach the top of their organizations. You should also be concerned that you don't become dysfunctional on the way up. As we get into the whys and wherefores, it might be helpful to keep in mind that these are not bad people, they are just dysfunctional managers.

Some are victims of the Peter Principle, which says that

organizations tend to promote people until they reach their level of incompetence. After that, they supposedly can't go any higher—that is, unless they have made friends with those higher up. In that case, they will continue moving up the ladder, because the old adage is true: It's not *what* they know, but *whom* they know that counts.

Not all dysfunctional executives reached the higher levels with help from their friends. Some got there in legitimate and often laudable ways, earning their advancement through hard work and sacrifice. But now that they have reached the top, they are burned out. They want to rest on their laurels. They already "gave it their best shot" and have no more to give.

Then there are those mentally gifted managers who were promoted because of their special knowledge and technical competence. Unfortunately, their unique skills have since become commonplace, and they are no longer needed. Managers like this are stuck at a level of "unconscious incompetence." In other words, they don't know what they don't know. And what's more, they probably don't care. They got theirs; why should they work any harder?

It is also important to realize that *you* may have contributed to the dysfunction at the top of your workplace. How so, you might ask. By withholding comments, criticisms, or concerns from those above you or by adding your own touch to information as it wends its way upward. This has become such a common practice that folks make a joke of it. You've no doubt seen Dilbert cartoons posted around the office, and you may even have a copy of the following comic handout that frequently materializes at planning sessions:

The Plan

In the beginning was the plan.
And then came the assumptions.
And the plan was without form,
And the assumptions without any substance,
And darkness was upon the face of all workers.
And they spake unto their team leaders, saying,
"Lo, this is a pail of dung, and none may abide the odor thereof."

And the team leaders went unto the supervisors and
saith,
"This new thing, it is a container of excrement, and
it is very strong, such that none may abide by it."
And the supervisors went unto their manager,
saying,
"This is a vessel of fertilizer, and none may abide its
strength."
And the manager went unto the vice president,
bearing this message:
"Lo, this plan contains that which aids plant growth,
and it is powerful."
And the vice president went unto the senior vice
president and saith,
"This new thing promoteth growth, and it is
powerful."
And the senior vice president went unto the
president and saith unto him,
"This powerful new plan will actively promote the
growth and efficiency of all units, even unto the
uttermost parts of the organization."
And the president looked upon the plan and saw that
it was good.
And "the plan" became policy.

—Author Unknown

People laugh when they read "The Plan" because it's funny, but it's also a sad commentary on life at the upper levels. Whoever said, "It's lonely at the top," must have been an executive in a dysfunctional workplace. If the bosses are setting their own course and steering the ship based on contaminated information from below, it's not totally their fault if the ship runs aground.

Information Flow

The two types of organization (functional and dysfunctional) referred to in previous chapters are depicted in Figure 8-1 as

Figure 8-1. The hourglass view of organizations.

hourglasses. An hourglass is a device that uses the flow of sand between an upper and a lower chamber to measure time. A narrow connecting link controls the flow between the chambers. Imagine the hourglass as your organization, with the sand representing information flowing from the upper level through the middle and into the lower levels.

What would happen at each level in your organization (upper, middle, and lower) if the information flow were inverted? In other words, what is the potential for information sharing? If information flows freely between the upper and lower levels, then you are in a functional organization (represented by the upright hourglass) that values planning. If, however, the information settles at both levels, then your organization is probably dysfunctional. In the dysfunctional example, the people at the upper and lower ends know what they know, but there is no flow between them. Planning, if there is any, is conducted in isolation.

The middle level of a functional organization is always under a lot of pressure—from above as the information comes down, again as it squeezes through, and finally as the response rebounds from below. The good news is that if you are in a functional setting, even when the information is under pressure, you can count on it to contain realistic time lines, reasonable goals, established priorities, measurable expectations, and a clear direction to follow.

Frustration is usually very high at both ends of the dysfunctional organization (depicted by the horizontal hourglass). Pressure from the lower chamber moves upward in the form of complaints, challenges, and concerns. Upper-level pressure moves downward in the form of directives, deadlines, and disciplinary action. In general, those in the middle of the hourglass know very little, but are expected to do a lot. If you identify with this description, then you probably feel that your hands are tied and there is nothing you can do. This is not the case. If you truly want to make a difference, you can. Later in this chapter you'll find out how.

In a dysfunctional organization, there is very little interest in formulating plans. What interest there is stems from a nagging concern that management *ought* to get something going. But until the dysfunctional organization discovers what it stands for, it will carry on as usual. You don't have to wait, however. You can develop your own action plan in preparation for the day when the organization makes its move—a plan that will provide the members of your team with the direction they seek. We'll have more to say about action planning later in this chapter.

Since we are using the hourglass as an example here, let's discuss *time.* A few years back, there was a big rush to manage time. Time management seminars and books all promoted the idea that if you tried harder, you could manage your time better. Most of the people attending a time management seminar were sent there by a boss who, according to the participants, was the one who really needed to be there. It didn't take long to see a connection between inefficient use of time and a dysfunctional manager.

When functional managers adopted time management techniques, their efficiency increased. Unfortunately, the introduction of the same techniques had the opposite effect on dysfunctional managers. The implementation of these innovations uncovered their lack of planning skills and their inability to cope with shorter time frames and multiple priorities.

As consumer scrutiny, economic uncertainty, and technological advances continue, dysfunctional managers will find it increasingly difficult to keep up. To overcome the negative effects of such a dysfunctional boss in your work setting, you must be the one who moves an idea through the stages of planning, research, development, production, and distribution. The planning wheel, shown in Figure 8-2, provides a way for you and your team to make up for the lack of higher-level direction.

The Planning Wheel

Dysfunctional executives tend to downplay the importance of the planning process. They claim that things are changing so fast that a plan would be out of date before it could be implemented. They avoid giving directions for similar reasons. Their real concern is to avoid the risks of failure. Their lack of direction setting has serious organizational consequences. An organization without direction also lacks policies, procedures, standards, goals, and objectives. Worst of all, there is no way of measuring productivity and performance other than by gut feeling.

Figure 8-2. The planning wheel.

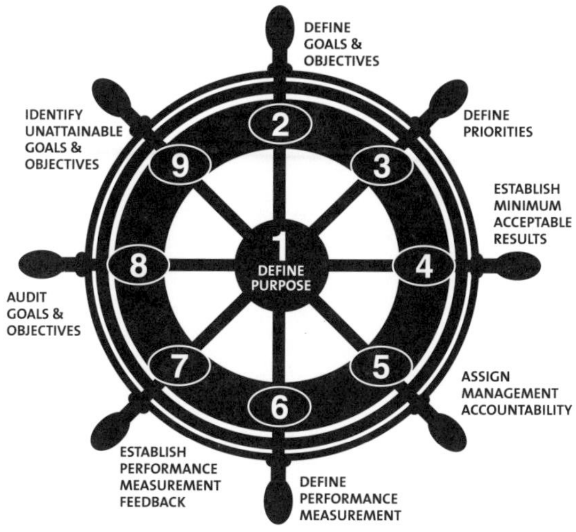

A formal planning process is needed to direct the actions of subordinates. Procedures, policies, and standards must be published and officially sanctioned. By having access to a planning process, you are in a position to select appropriate information for problem solving and decision making. Fortified with this knowledge, you are better able to provide direction to your crew.

An effective planning process must provide your crew with purpose and direction. If senior managers merely rely on the winds of fate as their guide, they may founder, run the ship aground, or be replaced. But until that happens, you can at least plot a course that accommodates the ever-changing winds and currents in your own area of responsibility.

The planning wheel (Figure 8-2) is a contemporary model resembling a ship's wheel. A ship's wheel controls the rudder, and therefore the direction, of the ship. At the center of the wheel is the hub, representing the purpose of the "cruise." Radiating outward from the hub are the spokes of the wheel. These spokes represent communication channels connecting the hub with the rim of the wheel. At the intersection of each spoke and the rim lies a point of action. Each point represents an opportunity for your team—your crew—to receive direction and report observations.

Before we take a closer look at the planning wheel, let's talk about why someone at your level should be interested in the planning process—a function usually reserved for upper management. Why bother, when it's not your job? Because, you might say, when the time comes, I want to know how to do it myself. Well, let me suggest that if you are in a dysfunctional workplace, there will be no better time than now to get started. Besides, it could improve your chances of moving upstairs where you can really do some good.

The Planning Components

1. *Define purpose.* Defining and maintaining a purpose is the most critical part of a successful planning strategy. By defining a purpose, you state who you are and what it is that you

do. If you don't have a clearly defined purpose, much time, talent, and treasure will be wasted while your team "does its own thing." To be effective, the planning strategy should provide your team with a charted vision and sense of direction, while at the same time remaining flexible and responsive to the challenge of change.

2. *Define goals and objectives.* Goals and objectives define the amount of work or number of tasks your team is expected to complete, the time team members need to spend doing it, the degree of accuracy they need to maintain, and the manner in which they should conduct themselves as they perform. Goals tell your team what the target is and how often the team is expected to hit it. Objectives give your followers a sense of direction and align them with your current understanding of the organization's purpose and direction.

3. *Define priorities.* Prioritizing establishes the importance of each goal and objective. It communicates to your team the order in which specific actions need to be taken. When resources are short and deadlines are pressing, a set of well-defined priorities enables your team to decide which goals matter the most and which can be set aside temporarily. Attaching priorities empowers your team to calculate the cost-benefit of alternative actions. Thus informed, your team can react to change quickly and smoothly by shifting priorities or setting new goals and objectives.

4. *Establish minimum acceptable results.* Setting minimum results is the basic element of the performance measurement process. Without a set of minimum standards, when pressured, your team is likely to let some vital tasks go while the team members focus on the highest priorities. Even though team members are doing their best and working hard, their efforts may be hindered by those elements that got the least attention. Failure to maintain minimum standards for each task is the primary source of bottlenecks, production stoppages, and work slowdowns. Knowing how to balance efforts between minimum results and high priorities is vital to your team's ability to achieve its goals and objectives.

5. *Assign management accountability.* If the goals and objectives that you are proposing did not originate with upper

management, you may have difficulty getting them approved. One way to expedite management accountability is to "assign" it yourself. Submit your carefully crafted plan to your boss with the stipulation that unless you are directed otherwise, you intend to move forward. The longer your boss ponders the issue of liability, the more time you have to prove the worthiness of your ideas. Once your boss sees the positive results, he or she is bound to step forward and make himself or herself accountable. After that, you are in a position to accept accountability if you know what will work, or to assign it to management if you need time to test your ideas.

6. *Define performance measurement.* Knowing what to focus on is the key to getting the results you expect from your team. Team members need to know how much time, talent, and treasure it will take to meet each performance goal. Also, they will want to know which indicators will be used to measure their performance. Hard indicators such as budget, quotas, errors, profits, sales, expenses, and deadlines can be applied to measure efficiency. Soft indicators such as satisfaction, experience, confidence, attitude, values, spirit, and motivation typically measure effectiveness.

7. *Establish performance measurement feedback.* Your team members want to know how they are doing. They are particularly interested in finding out when they are not meeting their performance objectives. To have meaning, feedback must be fair, objective, and timely. One way to ensure fairness is to involve more observers. If the report contains observations from coworkers, customers, suppliers, and employees in other departments, in addition to the supervisor, it covers "360 degrees" and provides an objective view. Timeliness is also important. It is simply a matter of providing feedback whenever a team member needs or wants to know how she or he is doing.

8. *Audit goals and objectives.* This is where you take a serious look at which goals and objectives are on schedule and which are behind. A review of performance expectations should also point out which goals and objectives were difficult to achieve and which were relatively easy. Separate those

goals that were beyond the skill levels of your team from those goals that were set too low. This is also a good time to uncover any dysfunctional side effects resulting from goal ambiguity or goal conflicts. Some team members may be stressed out from overload, while others may need greater challenges. Share your findings and provide recognition to those team members who met or exceeded their targets. Prepare corrective action plans for any team members whose results were lower than expected.

9. *Identify unattainable goals and objectives.* Take a close look at what's not working and try to decide what can be done to change the outcome. Pull your team together and discuss which goals and objectives are a waste of team members' time and energy. Decide whether these goals are worth any further investment. If attainment of a goal is still important, identify the constraints that are blocking success and find ways to remove these barriers or lessen the impact they are having on production.

Now that you understand how the planning wheel works, you can think of yourself as a planner. You may not be the one doing the planning, but you do know what to expect, and you can fill in the blanks if the folks upstairs leave anything out.

By the time you've worked your way around the planning wheel, the organization's purpose or your part in it may have altered slightly or even changed radically, depending upon the "winds of fate." If your purpose has changed, you may need to cease working on some goals and objectives. This is the best time to make a midcourse correction. By letting go of nonproductive activities, you can make room for new ones that better fit the revised purpose. Even if the purpose hasn't changed, it makes no sense to continue working on goals and objectives that are nonproductive. Your team will appreciate knowing that you are willing to let go of a goal when there is no reason to pursue it any further.

Confirming the Purpose

The action points around the rim of the planning wheel provide for the constant exchange and review of information.

This two-way communication system is what gives this planning model its flexibility. It allows the purpose of the "cruise," represented by the hub of the planning wheel, to be constantly reassessed in light of changing conditions. If warranted, the purpose can be altered before you proceed any further.

The wheel can be entered from any point on the rim. For instance, if you were assigned to manage a new team, you might plug into the planning wheel at stage 8 by looking at the team's current goals and objectives. If it has some, you can assess how well they are being performed and support the continuation of the work processes currently in place. If the team has no stated goals and objectives (which is likely to be the case in a dysfunctional setting), you can enter the planning wheel at stage 1 or 2. In either situation, it is important for you to make a good first impression. Gathering your new team around the planning wheel is a way to establish yourself as a leader and improve production simultaneously.

Peter Drucker, the prophetic management author, coined the axiom, "Don't do what you don't do." Whenever a job is not being done well or your team doesn't feel good about doing it, team members are probably doing something they don't do. Unless they have a clearly defined purpose, it is easy for them to get caught up in doing unproductive things because you don't know why they shouldn't. Information like this is not likely to be known at the upper levels. By understanding where your team fits in the overall plan, you are now in possession of information that can be useful to those higher up.

The primary reason for defining organizational purpose is to establish an essence—one that has meaning. Dysfunctional managers will try to implement change without knowing what it is they are trying to change. Functional managers know that the true challenge of change is understanding that you can't change it if you don't know what it is. Once a purpose is defined, it becomes a matter of harnessing the energy of external pressures to guide your team through the uncharted waters that lie ahead.

The relevance of defining a purpose was brought home to

me some years ago when I was asked to facilitate a problem-solving session for a Regional Girl Scout Council.

The problem? A rumor was going around that Girl Scout Cookies were contaminated with ground glass. The public panicked, and sales plummeted. The council was in deep financial trouble because it couldn't sell the cookies.

To be of any assistance, I first needed to know what the sale of cookies had to do with scouting. I began the first session by asking the council to define the purpose of selling Girl Scout Cookies. Without hesitation, they each in turn made the same declaration: "to raise money." I then suggested that they could raise a lot of money by selling marijuana door-to-door.

"Think of it," I announced. "You've got a distribution network already set up. And the cops couldn't possibly arrest all those little girls." I finished by suggesting that they'd make a fortune in no time. Their problem would be solved.

You can imagine their reaction. Stunned by my suggestion, their faces registered shock, disgust, and dismay. They were livid with anger—all directed at me. The chairwoman demanded to know how I could suggest something so sinister. She and her colleagues ranted and raved for quite some time, expounding at length on the reputation of scouting, the standing their organization had in the community, and the values they were trying to instill in the girls. Eventually they realized what they were saying. After a moment's silence, they broke out in sheepish grins. They had grasped my point. Shortly after that, they huddled in small groups and set about to more clearly define their purpose.

In doing so, they also came up with an ingenious plan to rejuvenate cookie sales. They now understood that the purpose of selling cookies was to present the girls to the public as products of the scouting program, and to give people an opportunity to contribute to their program through the purchase of cookies. Once they defined their purpose, it wasn't difficult to solve the problem. Since the public loved the cookies and was avoiding them only out of fear, all the council had to do was calm that fear to improve sales.

So the girls went back out door-to-door, but with an added touch to their sales routine. When folks answered their doorbell, they'd find one of the scouts on their porch happily munching on a cookie. People could see for themselves that the cookies were safe to eat. Did the plan work? You bet. Cookie sales for that year far exceeded expectations.

9

Adjusting to Change

Consider for a moment the businesses, schools, government agencies, hospitals, churches, and charities you have worked for, worked with, contributed to, been a client of, or received services from during the past few years. These organizations come in a variety of shapes and sizes. They provide a wide assortment of goods and services. Some are well run, while others barely get by. Whatever their status, it is just a matter of time before every one of them, and the people they employ, must change what they do or risk losing your patronage. Some will change willingly, others reluctantly. Yet all will do so or they won't be around much longer.

Downsizing, rightsizing, reengineering, reinventing—these are all internal adjustments to external changes. As economic and social conditions continue to fluctuate, managers will be under continuing pressure to be flexible and responsive. People in leadership roles like yours will be expected to foresee the need to change and to make on-the-job adjustments without losing momentum. Unfortunately, the introduction of change, even in a functional work environment, starts people guessing. It produces ambiguity and inconsistency—the building blocks of dysfunction in the workplace.

In this chapter, we will explore those dynamics. We'll

start by looking at how organizational misalignment can have an impact on you and your team, and what you can do when it does.

Organizational Alignment

An organization can structure itself in three basic ways. Each of these structures is determined by the four factors shown in Figure 9-1. An organization is properly aligned or functional when all of the factors defining it are in the same column. For example, let's assume that Company X is a bottom-line organization. Its *goal* is to make a profit, its *function* is to increase productivity, its *relationships* are contractual, and the *problems* facing management mostly concern efficiency, e.g., cutting costs, increasing production, upgrading equipment, and so on. An organization becomes misaligned and potentially dysfunctional whenever the factors defining it are taken from different columns. For example, let's say that Company X wanted to maintain a stable, loyal workforce and could afford to provide great benefits to attract people who were will-

Figure 9-1. Organizational alignment.

	BOTTOM LINE	MIDDLE LINE	TOP LINE
GOALS	PROFIT	PROFIT & HUMAN CARE	PROFIT & SERVICE
FUNCTIONS	INCREASE PRODUCTIVITY	LOYALTY	VISIONARY
RELATIONSHIPS	CONTRACT	FAMILY & VALUES	IDEALS
PROBLEMS	EFFICIENCY	COMMUNICATION	MEANING OF THINGS

ing to make a long-term commitment. In other words, the company began to move toward a middle-line form. Then suddenly the company experienced a couple of bad years and was forced to let some people go and cut the benefits of those who stayed. By moving toward the middle-line form and then withdrawing, it has created a misalignment that may harm it for years.

Misalignment is most likely to occur during periods of change, when some or all of the factors are mixed. By mixing the factors, an organization creates ambiguity, which can lead to inconsistency—the first and second stages of dysfunction.

As we examine the four factors that influence organizational structure, be thinking about which form most closely describes your workplace. Also make note of any current or potential misalignment. Even though you may not be in a position to do anything to change the current form, later on we'll discuss your options and ways to cope with whatever misalignment you discover.

1. *Goals* define the reason the organization exists.
2. *Functions* determine what management's role should be.
3. *Relationships* define how employees connect to the organization.
4. *Problems* refer to the issues facing the organization.

The Bottom-Line Organization

Goal = Profit

The bottom-line organization has one driving purpose: to make a profit. Managers are charged with reducing costs and increasing income. Decisions are based on rate of return for the investors. New employees are hired and new equipment is purchased only after management demonstrates that such actions will improve profits.

Function = Increase Productivity

The role of management is to raise the level of performance and productivity without adding to the cost of the product or service. Operating hours, production schedules, and distribution strategies are based on pushing more out the door. Emphasis is placed on speed and volume. Research and development are limited. Product lines and services are discontinued if they don't sell well.

Relationship = Contract

Wages, vacations, benefits, job security, and promotions are based on how much each employee contributes to the bottom line. Employees are expected to be at work on time and to work hard while they are there. Discipline is tight, and rules are strictly enforced. Overtime and layoffs are based on the needs of the organization. The performance appraisal and reward systems focus on constant improvement.

Problem = Efficiency

Doing more with less is the common theme in the bottom-line organization. Managers focus on eliminating mistakes and improving quality. High rates of employee turnover are expected. Employees are hired at entry level and trained on the job. Supervisors balance simultaneous demands for quality and quantity. Rewards are given for ideas and suggestions that improve the bottom line.

The Middle-Line Organization

Goals = Profit and Human Care

The middle-line organization looks at people as the most important factor in making a profit. Growth and development of employees are closely aligned with organizational objectives so that both will be together for the long haul. Middle-line organizations are concerned with how people fit in to the organization's culture. Training and development are important recruiting and retention factors.

Function = Loyalty

Building allegiance is important to management. Keeping employees happy and satisfying their needs are key features of the middle-line organization. The views and opinions of long-term employees are sought as part of the decision-making process. Those who hung in there during the bad times are highly respected as the pillars of the organization.

Relationships = Family and Values

Employees are encouraged to view the organization as their extended family. Managers help people resolve personal problems. Group norms are established and used as guides for work behaviors. Longevity awards and acknowledgment of birthdays, illnesses, deaths, marriages, and anniversaries contribute to the family atmosphere. New employees participate in orientation programs designed to make them feel welcome and to acquaint them with the ways of the workplace family.

Problem = Communication

Keeping employees fully informed is management's primary responsibility. Employees expect notification of such things as safety hazards, production records, sales totals, and promotion opportunities to appear on bulletin boards and in company-sponsored newsletters. Managers are expected to develop two-way communication systems that provide adequate, timely, helpful, and accurate information.

The Top-Line Organization

Goals = Profit and Service

Top-line organizations have clearly defined missions, and their objectives are supported by the community they serve. Meeting the needs of large, public groups is the primary motive of the top-line organization. Profit becomes the basis for providing a needed public service. Managers are responsible for identifying new funding sources and planning new programs to serve larger populations.

Function = Visionary

The leadership challenge is to decide what the organization should do in the future. Exhaustive methods are used to gather information, conduct research, identify trends, and forecast future growth needs. Managers are proactive innovators who meet frequently to discuss predictions, hopes, and preferences relating to the future of their organization.

Relationship = Ideals

People are attracted to the top-line organization because they want to make a difference in the lives of others. Employees are motivated by a common belief that what they are doing is important to the greater community. The opportunity to participate in a worthy cause is more important than promotions or higher salaries.

Problem = Meaning of Things

Managers come together frequently to identify and resolve important issues. Before a resolution is proposed, alternatives are explored in terms of what each might mean to the people involved. Top-line organizations adhere to the principles of enlightened self-awareness to ensure that everyone understands and appreciates the consequences of his or her actions.

Organizational Misalignment

There have always been organizational realignments during economic downturns, technological changeovers, and national market shifts. Layoffs, cutbacks, and plant closings are not new to the workplace. But it seems that in recent years, organizational misalignment has been happening more frequently and is leaving a deeper, more negative impression. One reason may be that most employees expect companies to function like middle-line organizations. After all, we have been conditioned to expect employers to supply jobs that meet our needs. But in today's unpredictable market, major employers and business owners are sometimes forced to become bottom-line companies just to survive.

There is nothing wrong with being a bottom-line company, if the company is properly aligned and this is clearly communicated. But when management says one thing, yet does another, the organization is misaligned and potentially dysfunctional. A common example is a bottom-line company portraying itself as middle-line. Then you might have the chief executive officer professing that people are the company's most important asset, even though the company hires mostly part-time employees, offers limited benefits, pays wages below prevailing rates, and lays people off when things are slow.

Any organization pretending to be something it is not is misaligned and will eventually become dysfunctional. For example, bottom-line companies that are masquerading as middle-line companies might promise long-term employment, growth opportunities, career planning, advanced training, and profit sharing. Should their profit projections not hold up, however, they quickly shift their focus to the bottom line to cut costs. The longer-term, higher-skilled employees are the first to be cut because their wages are higher. This maneuver forces the remaining, less-experienced employees to work longer and harder. Overtime goes up, and quality goes down. Production declines because people are afraid to say anything for fear of losing their jobs. These tactics are referred to in management jargon as "getting lean and mean" or "doing more with less." The net result in the short term may be an improved bottom line, but in the long term, it adds to the dysfunction in the workplace.

So, why am I telling you all this? Even if you wanted to, you couldn't do anything about it, right? Not true—there's lots you can do. In the first place, just knowing what's behind the dysfunction should make you feel better. After all, you're not crazy—this stuff is really happening. Second, if you understand what's driving the change, you'll be able to help those around you who are having difficulty adjusting to it. Finally, if you can recognize the signs of creeping dysfunction, you'll be able to overcome it before it gains momentum.

It is amazing how fast a misaligned organization can move through the first two stages of dysfunction and get locked into the third stage, where the existence of ambiguity and inconsistency is undiscussable. Should the misalignment continue, it won't take very long before the fourth stage is reached. The following are summary examples of real organizations heading for the fourth stage of dysfunction.

As you read these true stories, put yourself in the shoes of your counterparts and think about how you might have reacted in the same circumstances. Also think about what problems you'd have to face if these situations were to occur in your organization. It's a risk-free opportunity to practice with somebody else's problems. Who knows, someday you may find yourself in a similar situation, and what you learn here might help.

1. Manufacturer

This large, growth-oriented company with plants located worldwide and $1 billion in sales had for years posed as a middle-line organization. The president personally encouraged employees to seek increased responsibility, promising promotions and bonuses for those willing to move up the ladder. However, none of those who received them could explain to me what they did to earn their bonuses and pay raises. Sometimes they were based on individual performance. Other times they were tied to sales or safety or customer satisfaction. For undisclosed reasons, the president had been known to withhold or cut bonuses to an entire plant. Some managers who relocated at the president's urging were left out of the bonus awards at their new plant. The word got around to avoid start-ups because the company didn't give bonuses or pay raises until a new plant turned a profit—an average of three years. The employees at one of the best-run plants were expecting a big bonus because they had been tops in every category in which a bonus had been previously awarded. The management team was certain that it had all the bases covered. But it was not to be. That year there were no bonuses or raises. Instead, the owner of this family-run business decided to make a multimillion-dollar, tax-deductible contribution to his favorite charity. As the long-term employees finally accepted the realization that they were just part of the bottom line, both morale and production plummeted.

2. Health Care Organization

As the local competition for registered nurses heated up, the bottom-line thinkers at this otherwise middle-line hospital came up with a revolutionary cost-saving strategy. They proposed to lower the salaries of their staff nurses and, in return, provide 100 percent health insurance coverage. That way, the hospital would come out ahead financially and the nurses would be "tied to the organization for the long term." The hospital spokesperson rationalized that if the hospital cut base pay and gave the nurses a more generous insurance plan than the competition, its staff nurses wouldn't want to (make that couldn't afford to) seek employment elsewhere. Part 2 of this scheme included a cash sign-up bonus to attract nurses from the competing hospitals. This inducement, coupled with the increased benefits, was supposed to resolve the nursing shortage. It didn't. Instead, it made the situation worse. The staff nurses felt less loyalty to the hospital, not more. And, as professional caregivers, they strongly resented being treated like a commodity. As the bottom line came into focus, morale declined steadily and the nursing shortage worsened.

3. Service Provider

This nonprofit service provider had built a reputation as a top-line organization. It had little difficulty attracting talented employees and top-notch managers who willingly accepted lower salaries in exchange for an opportunity to serve their community—that is, until the newly elected board president, a bottom-line business owner, convinced the board to set its sights higher. According to his reasoning, the organization had to attract a higher-caliber staff—and to do so, it had to pay higher salaries. On the basis of the wage and salary figures he introduced as "evidence," this would mean a 20 percent increase. Despite warnings from the executive director and the organization's accountant, the board, pushed by the president, forged ahead. The new salaries were set and the final costs calculated—and the board found itself facing a huge budget deficit. Again the president looked to the bottom line for the solution. The organization would still raise the salaries, but to balance the budget, it would simultaneously cut its contribution to employee health insurance premiums. The board was delighted with its efficiency. The employees were not. The higher pay rates increased their taxes. The combination of higher taxes and higher insurance premiums resulted in a net *loss* of pay. The executive director and several key staffers resigned in protest. By making pay an issue, the board had undermined the staff's motivation to serve. According to the departing director, "They took away the specialness of working here." Following this episode, the organization became even more dysfunctional. The board president split the board into those who supported him and those who didn't. More employees left. There are several lawsuits pending for back wages and unfair dismissals, and, sadly, the pool of volunteers has all but disappeared. The greater good of the community will no doubt suffer.

Successful Strategies

Organizational misalignment can also occur by design, when an organization purposefully realigns itself to face the challenge of change head-on. For example, in preparation for restructuring or downsizing, management may intentionally shift from a middle-line to a bottom-line structure while deciding how best to cut costs and whom to lay off. In these cases, the dysfunctional impact of organizational misalignment can be minimized by the formation of a transition monitoring team as discussed in Chapter 6.

The following are three examples of organizations that deliberately realigned themselves in an effort to refocus their mission or redesign their organization. In each case, management intentionally engineered the change. A transition monitoring team was formed to facilitate the process and to be alert for dysfunctional behaviors. The organizations cited in the first and second examples were forced into realignment during a period of economic struggle. In the third example, an inspirational leader saw the need for change and realigned her organization to meet the challenge head-on.

1. Public Agency

The economic downturn that began in the early 1990s was particularly difficult for small municipalities that depended upon tourists for tax revenue. In this resort city, the city council, city manager, and department heads had worked together for years and had become a very strong team. This was clearly a middle-line organization in every respect. The employees were long-term and considered themselves members of one big family. Though everyone tried to maintain a positive attitude as the tourist trade continued to decline, it soon became evident that the level of city staffing would have to be cut. Council members went into the community to explain the situation and gain support for service reductions. Management developed a plan to become a bottom-line organization, at least while it dealt with the current budget shortfall. To minimize the dysfunction associated with the realignment, a transition monitoring team was formed. For the first time in the city's history, staffing was reduced. Each of the fourteen people who lost their jobs was provided with assistance in locating a new job in the community. It was a very painful experience, but it was handled in as gentle a manner as one could hope for under the circumstances. The city manager later described his feelings about the downsizing. He said it was like telling his four children that because he could only afford to keep three, one of them would have to find another family.

2. Medical Enterprise

In the mid-1980s, I had the privilege of consulting with a group of physicians who put together a truly unique medical center. It was not only the first such endeavor, but the largest facility of its kind in the world. The founders were determined to build a top-line organization that would have a world-class reputation for medical excellence, state-of-the-art technology, and unsurpassed diagnostic services. This was achieved through teamwork and constant training on the part of everyone involved. Since then, however, the center has downsized twice, eventually cutting the workforce almost in half. Without question, the decision makers shifted to the middle line first in an attempt to keep the "family" together because they truly cared about their employees. That reengineering effort kept them afloat for another six months. But conditions worsened, and they were forced to shift to the bottom line in order to survive. A transition monitoring team was formed to help the staff cope with the stress of losing 25 percent of the family during the first reduction. Six months later, the transition team was reformed to minimize the dysfunction when a second layoff affected another 15 percent of the family. This organization and the people it employs are currently holding on by sheer determination and their desire to remain a top-notch service provider. They still keep one eye on the bottom line, but they are slowly moving toward the middle line again.

Note: After the first layoff, the managing partners met with the remaining staff to answer their questions about the organization's future. The first question came as a surprise to management. One employee wanted to know when he would get a pay raise. He reasoned that with a 25 percent smaller staff, he would have to work harder, and therefore he deserved more money.

3. County Government

This is an example of an organization that started out as middle line, then shifted to bottom line, and is currently striving to become top line. Not surprisingly, this series of realignments has stirred up a lot of dysfunction. Not everyone wanted to leave the security of the small "family" that had worked together for many years. Under previous administrators, the workload had increased, but the quality had not. The staff blamed management, and the managers criticized each other. Then, along came a new administrator who said that they could and would do better. She outlined her plans to enlarge the customer base and provide higher-quality services to the taxpayers. This, at least in her mind, was no longer going to be a typical bureaucratic agency. This agency had a federal mandate to fulfill, and she was going to provide the vision to do it. In the process, she would raise the expectations of everyone in this organization. Thus began a five-year commitment to improve quality and increase productivity. Within two years the agency got state-of-the-art computers, the staff was nearly doubled, and the performance goals increased. Shifting from middle line to bottom line was easy. All the agency had to do was concentrate on efficiency and productivity. Shifting focus to the top line has turned out to be much harder. Only a limited number of employees embraced the notion of serving the greater community. Nearly a third of the workforce resisted the idea. The remaining majority waited to see who would provide the energy and leadership to move the organization into the future.

A transition monitoring team had been formed earlier on, but it soon took on a more influential role as the Training Council, a powerful body responsible for all training and development within the agency. As the realignment continued, the Training Council provided new employee orientation programs, plus management coaching and team interventions to minimize individual and organizational dysfunction in the workplace.

Making Adjustments

As children, many of us were led to believe that if we studied hard in school, we would get a good job with a good company and earn a good living. Whenever the extended family gathered around the dinner table, we heard how grandpa had worked in the same job with the same company until he retired. Aunt Ruth recalled her retirement dinner, when the school board honored her for twenty-five years of devoted service. My father retired after thirty-seven years with the same organization. But now, as the economy changes and organizations struggle to realign themselves, the notion of steady employment with the same company doesn't ring true anymore.

Since people tend to draw their sense of purpose, meaning, and value from their workplace, the first place to look for signs of organizational dysfunction is within your team. If team members claim to be discouraged, disappointed, or disillusioned, yet can't come up with specifics, they could be feeling the effects of a misalignment. Once you recognize the symptoms, you can take steps to counter them. You can minimize much of your team's anxiety over change by helping members make the appropriate adjustments. You might want to review the transition monitoring list in Chapter 6, and think of ways to adapt them on a smaller scale for your team alone.

Upper-level management is responsible for communicating the purpose of an organizational change and its intentions for the future. Unfortunately, senior managers are often distracted by the pressure of the situation and are unaware of how quickly misalignment can create dysfunction. When communication from the upper levels is sparse, it is critical that you interpret how the factors depicted in Figure 9-1 influence the way your team is coping with the misalignment.

Adjusting to change can be rough for those who need a steady path to follow. In the event that your organization is misaligned, you can still guide your team in a positive direction. Should your organization subsequently become dysfunctional, you may be the only person capable of providing your team with a proper sense of relevance and purpose.

10

Influencing Work Behaviors

One of the ways to uncover the leadership potential in an organization is to bring the hourly workers together and ask them questions. Lower-level employees tend to respond more freely when grouped together. Because they are seldom asked for their opinion, they are usually more than happy to share it with someone from outside the organization.

When I am given the opportunity to be with lower-level employees, I make an effort to discover what type of people they view as leaders, and why. Getting answers to this question is easy if it is posed in a nonthreatening manner. For example, I might ask them to think about all the people they have ever worked for in their lives. I give them a few moments to ponder this. Then I ask them which of those people would they gladly work for again, and why. I don't ask for names, just for the reasoning behind their choices. Their answers usually fall into two extremes. One group likes a leader who gives them an idea of what he wants and lets them figure out how to get it done. Opposing that perspective are those who prefer a leader who tells them exactly what she expects and gives them clear directions on how to accomplish it. From this exercise, the employees discover that different people respond to leadership in different ways. This leads us into a discussion of leadership practices in functional and dysfunctional organizations.

Have you ever wondered why some employees react to your directions precisely, while others disregard most of what you say? Have you ever noticed that some employees ask you what to do, while others know what to do without asking? How about those employees who will run with an idea and make it work, while others must know how it works before they even try it? Now think for a minute about which of these types you prefer to manage. And while you're thinking, try to remember a time before you supervised people. You may recall that in those days you dealt mostly with two types of people—those who were compatible with you and those who weren't. The basis for compatibility was either a preference for the person (social interaction) or the way that person worked with you (task interaction), or both. This is often referred to as personality or behavioral style.

In the workplace, we find a variety of different personalities and behaviors. Some people like to study any given situation before they do something about it. Others prefer to do something about the situation and then study what happens. Your way of getting things done may not fit with the way I might handle it. When it doesn't matter, either way will suffice. Therefore, as long as we each have the choice and are allowed to act independently, we are likely to have a functional relationship. That changes if we are required to work together. Then one of us will try to influence the other's way of doing things. My preferred work behavior might not be acceptable to you, and vice versa. Unless we can agree on a common strategy, you might try to force me to change my behavior, and I might bring the same pressure to bear on you.

In a functional workplace, we could look to the supervisor for leadership or to other members of our team to help us reach a mutually acceptable resolution. (The importance of maintaining a neutral environment was one of the tenets of teamwork presented in Chapter 4.) In a dysfunctional setting, the lack of team support or the absence of influential leadership will force us to struggle for control. Left on our own, you might become aggressive and I might withdraw in response.

Or I might meet your aggressive behavior with a force of my own, so that whichever of us had the stronger influence would prevail. For example, if you had a political connection to my supervisor, you could more easily engineer a change in my work behavior. But every time we worked together after that, I would feel antagonistic. As a result, our job performance would decline, our personal relationship would suffer, and our work environment would not remain neutral for long. Our inability to get along, coupled with a lack of leadership, would force those around us to take sides or to avoid working with either of us, thus creating an ambiguous situation that would eventually lead to inconsistent outcomes. If the ambiguity was not questioned (stage 1) and the resulting inconsistencies were ignored (stage 2), we would be creating dysfunction in our workplace.

Behaviorial Patterns

In his book *The Emotions of Normal People,* William Moulton Marston established a link between environmental influences and behavior patterns. During the 1920s, Marston developed a model of human behavior that suggested that people tend to behave differently in *favorable* (supportive) situations from the way they do in *antagonistic* (pressure) situations. To better understand how we are going to use Marston's model in this chapter, think of *favorable* as functional and *antagonistic* as dysfunctional.

Marston was interested in determining how emotional states influenced behavior. His research resulted in the discovery of "four integrative principles of primary emotions: dominance **(D)**, compliance **(C)**, submission **(S)**, and inducement **(I)**." Marston and his associates incorporated these four principles into a four-factor model that explains emotional behavior. Later, industrial psychologists developed training tools and profiles that provided a wider application of Marston's principles.

I frequently administer these tools to help managers and coworkers better understand how they interact with one another in the workplace. When I am working in a dysfunctional environment, there is one particular instrument that I prefer. Carlson Learning Company (800-777-9897) publishes a unique forced-choice instrument called the Personal Profile System. The profile is self-administered, self-scored, and self-interpreted. This (self) format ensures that respondents don't need anyone to tell them what the results mean. Also, they are not confronted with information that is difficult to understand, and, best of all, they don't have to disclose what the profile says about them. The contents of the profile are presented in a positive way. There are no "scores," only measures of intensity and descriptions of behaviors. This feature is very helpful for dysfunctional employees, who are frequently worried about "not passing the test." These are some of the many reasons I recommend this particular profile as a training tool in a dysfunctional workplace.*

The Personal Profile System, also know as the DiSC Profile, is based on Marston's four primary behavioral dimensions, redefined as dominance **(D)**, influence **(i)**, steadiness **(S)**, and conscientiousness **(C)**. It is the combination of these four dimensions, shown in Figure 10-1, coupled with the organizational environment, that influences how people behave in the workplace. The primary tendencies associated with each of these dimensions are highlighted below.

Behavioral Dimensions

Dominance

The emphasis is on shaping the environment by overcoming opposition to accomplish results. People with this behavioral trait desire an environment that includes power and

*In addition to the Personal Profile System described here, many other excellent assessment tools such as the Myers-Briggs Type Indicator, The Leadership Practices Inventory, The Parker Team Player Survey, and The Personal Style Inventory are available from reputable training resource companies.

Figure 10-1. Behavioral styles.

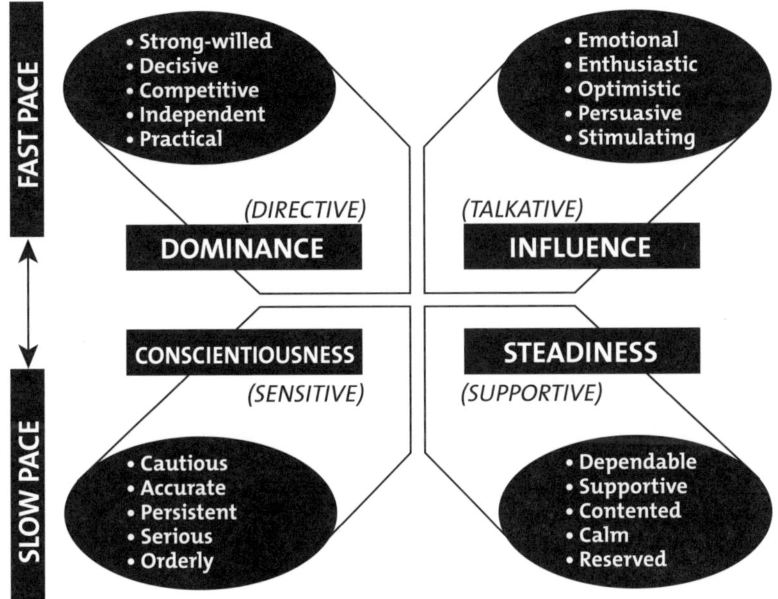

authority, prestige and challenge, and opportunity for individual accomplishments. Primary tendencies include:

- Getting immediate results
- Causing action
- Accepting challenges

Influence

The emphasis is on shaping the environment by influencing or persuading others. People with this behavioral trait desire an environment that includes popularity, social recognition, public recognition of ability, and freedom of expression. Primary tendencies include:

- Contacting people
- Making a favorable impression
- Verbalizing with articulateness

Steadiness

The emphasis is on cooperating with others to carry out the task. People with this behavioral trait desire an environment that includes maintenance of the status quo unless they are given reasons for change, predictable routines, and credit for work accomplished. Primary tendencies include:

- Performing in a consistent, predictable manner
- Demonstrating patience
- Developing specialized skills

Conscientiousness

The emphasis is on working conscientiously within existing circumstances to ensure quality and accuracy. People with this behavioral trait desire an environment that includes clearly defined performance expectations, placement of value on quality and accuracy, and a reserved, businesslike atmosphere. Primary tendencies include:

- Attention to key directives and standards
- Concentrating on key details
- Thinking analytically, weighing pros and cons

Note: The above information was gleaned from the Personal Profile System.*

Behavioral Strengths and Limitations

When you look at these descriptions, it becomes apparent that all four behavioral dimensions are needed in a functional workplace. In building a team, it is important to consider the strengths of each dimension. As a manager, blending these

*Adapted from the Personal Profile System®, ©Copyright 1994, Carlson Learning Company, Minneapolis, Minnesota. Used with permission of Carlson Learning Company.

strengths into a working team is your job. In a functional organization, pulling people together to form a team can be an exciting and rewarding experience. The following is a list of the functional qualities that each dimension brings to your team:

- *Dominance:* removing roadblocks to the team's success
- *Influence:* building morale and unity within the team
- *Steadiness:* working out the team's plans and strategies
- *Conscientiousness:* keeping track of how the team is doing

When people are not under pressure, they have time to socialize their responses. That is, they will say what they think needs to be said, and they will say it in a socially acceptable manner. But when they are pushed, they may behave very differently. Being under pressure brings out their reactive nature. Employees may respond in much the same way as they reacted to pressure as a child. Consequently, dysfunctional behaviors are more likely to emerge under pressure than at any other time. While some people excel under pressure, others cave in, lash out, or withdraw.

The enough-is-never-enough attitude that prevails in a dysfunctional workplace, coupled with the pressures created by the need for continuous improvement and the demands for higher performance, are the main sources of stress. The pressure from stress brings our basic fears to the surface. Once these fears are uncovered, they tend to influence how we behave.

Under pressure, people often drop their socialized responses and shift to their natural, less controlled behavior. In other words, when "push comes to shove," some people react by pushing and shoving. In a functional environment, this shift in behavior is temporary and easy to influence. However, in a dysfunctional environment, these behavioral changes tend to last longer and are therefore more difficult to influence.

The following list provides a vivid description of the basic fears and traits for each behavioral dimension. Included are suggestions for influencing a positive behavioral change. If you understand what happens to people under pressure, you will be in a better position to influence their behavior positively.

Limitations Under Pressure

Dominance

Basic fears are loss of control, boredom, restrictions, being taken advantage of, slowness, and being viewed as too soft on others.

People with this trait tend to:

* Stimulate anxiety in others.
* Sulk when not in the limelight.
* Be critical and find fault.
* Resist participation as part of a team.

Methods of Influence

To minimize dysfunctional behavior and help create a more functional environment, consider the following:

1. Provide direct answers—be clear, specific, brief, and to the point.
2. Stick to business—be prepared with requirements, objectives, and support materials.
3. If you disagree, take issue with the facts, not the person.
4. Motivate and persuade by referring to objectives and results.

Influence

Basic fears are social rejection, loss of status, looking bad to others, a fixed environment, and complex relationships.

People with this trait tend to:

* Act impulsively—heart over mind.
* Draw inconsistent conclusions.
* Make decisions solely on gut feelings.
* Have difficulty planning and estimating time.

Methods of Influence

To minimize dysfunctional behavior and help create a more functional environment, consider the following:

1. Provide opportunities for these people to verbalize about ideas, people, and their intuition.
2. Don't deal with excessive details; put things in writing; pin them to modes of action.
3. Provide testimonials from people they see as important, prominent.
4. Offer special, immediate, and extra incentives for their willingness to take risks.

Steadiness

Basic fears are loss of stability, inferior work standards, dissension or conflict, selling abstract ideas, change, and disorganization.

People with this trait tend to:

* Have trouble meeting multiple deadlines.
* Need help getting started on new assignments.
* Continue to do things the way they have always been done.
* Wait for orders before acting.

Methods of Influence

To minimize dysfunctional behavior and help create a more functional environment, consider the following:

1. Show sincere interest in them; find areas of common involvement; be candid and open.

2. Present your case softly and nonthreateningly. Ask "how" questions to get their opinion.
3. Patiently draw out personal goals and work with them to help achieve these goals.
4. Give them time to adjust to new ideas or departures from current practices.

Conscientiousness

Basic fears are lack of conformity, criticism of their work, irrational acts, ridicule, antagonism, and being too predictable.

People with this trait tend to:

* Hesitate to act without precedent.
* Get bogged down in decision making.
* Want a full explanation before changes are made.
* Yield positions to avoid controversy.

Methods of Influence

To minimize dysfunctional behavior and help create a more functional environment, consider the following:

1. Give them time to verify the predictability of your actions; be accurate and realistic.
2. If you disagree, make an organized presentation of your position and ask for their input.
3. Implement actions with a step-by-step timetable; assure them there won't be surprises.
4. Build your credibility by listing pros and cons for any suggestion you make.

Note: The information provided in this section was taken from the Personal Profile System Facilitator's Manual.*

*Adapted from the Personal Profile System® Facilitator's Kit, ©Copyright 1994, Carlson Learning Company, Minneapolis. Used with permission of Carlson Learning Company.

Influential Leadership

How you handle work behaviors will be watched very closely. Let me explain by sharing this story.

I was once called in to a construction company that was having difficulty finding and keeping a skilled labor pool. In addition to losing people, it had also lost a couple of lawsuits filed by former employees. As if that weren't enough, its relationship with the trade unions wasn't too hot, either. Something had to be done.

I was invited to meet with the managers to introduce myself and to talk with them about their problems. At the beginning of the meeting, they denied having any problems. Then a quiet voice suggested that I was talking to the wrong people. This prompted a second person to point toward the personnel director. I was about to ask the director a question, when an angry manager jumped up and said he would tell me exactly what was wrong. I encouraged him to continue. He did.

"Why, just the other day," he began, "I sent two of the new hires out to dig a trench." He went on to explain that he had instructed them to use only shovels. In other words, they were supposed to dig the trench by hand, rather than by machine. "How hard can that be?" he pleaded. Encouraged by his colleagues, he launched into a tirade against personnel for hiring such "nitwits."

It turned out that when these two guys got to the job site, they realized that it would take them all day to do the job with shovels, so they decided to use a mechanical backhoe to get the job done more quickly. Unfortunately, the backhoe ripped into an underground telephone cable. The damage was extensive, and so were the repair costs. As the manager finished recounting this story, he triumphantly announced that he had since fired both of those "fools."

I couldn't pass up this opportunity to probe a little deeper. I asked the still-fuming manager if he had known about the telephone cable beforehand. "Sure," he said. "That's why I told them to use hand tools. I figured they'd find the cable and dig around it." I pushed him a little by suggesting that the broken cable could have been avoided had he told the two workers what he knew. "That's none of their business!" he bellowed. "I told them what to do. People who can't follow orders shouldn't get hired."

For the rest of the meeting I listened to the managers moan about terrible employees, damaged equipment, and safety violations. In each case, the personnel director was blamed for hiring "such nitwits." It was clear that these managers accepted no responsibility for the recruitment and retention problems.

An influential leader, unlike the manager in the backhoe story, must accept responsibility for the actions of her or his followers. Before people will follow you, they must understand what you expect of them. They also need to know the best way to interact with you and with others on their team. Functional employees can figure out who you are and determine for themselves how best to work with you. Dysfunctional employees don't fully understand their own actions, so don't expect them to give much constructive thought to anyone else's.

So, you might ask, why waste time on dysfunctional employees? Why not leave them alone and concentrate solely on the functional workers? You can do that, and it will work, as long as your organization doesn't change. You may recall from Chapter 6 that dysfunction is most easily exposed when an organization undergoes change. Let's look at why this happens.

Organizations that are experiencing a period of growth or a downsizing will usually try to take advantage of their situation. Seasoned managers view staffing reallocations as good opportunities to move their best people into key positions and get rid of the "deadwood." Research into the aftereffects of organizationwide changes, such as an expansion or a downsizing, points to a chilling conclusion: Deadwood *floats.* When dysfunctional employees hear about a staffing change, they immediately focus on keeping their jobs.

Functional people have an external network that keeps them in touch with job openings. They also have the confidence to look beyond their current employer. As competitors get wind of their availability, the best people are often hired away. Dysfunctional people aren't confident enough to look elsewhere, which is why no one from the outside offers them a job.

As the change takes shape, a shadow competition begins to unfold between the functional and dysfunctional employees. The term *shadow* is used because management is usually in the dark about what is really happening. There are several behaviors that will tip you off to when and why such a competition is taking place. (Review the rumors section of Chapter 6.)

Dysfunctional employees will stand together in pointing out the faults and failures of their functional competitors. One common technique is for two of them to hang around after a meeting, hoping to catch you alone. When they do, one will say, "Have you got a minute?" Once they have you cornered, they claim that it is hard for them to say something negative about a star performer, but they thought you ought to know that so-and-so has been looking for another job. They reluctantly share the names of others who are more concerned for themselves than for the organization. They usually finish with a personal declaration of loyalty and an offer to take on more work if necessary. These dysfunctional employees are hoping to gain your favor while casting doubt on the high performers. Meanwhile, the functional folks are updating their résumés and looking for better opportunities elsewhere.

Because dysfunctional employees have more at stake in staying put, they are more likely to fight for their jobs. As you try to influence their behavior, remember that you are dealing with deep-seated feelings and fears. Dysfunctional people can cover up their fears and hold their feelings in check when things are going their way. But those fears are always waiting to crop up when these people are antagonized. When pushed to respond to ambiguity and inconsistency, dysfunctional employees become fearful that their personal shortfalls will be exposed. They must trust you to treat them fairly if they do make mistakes. In their eyes, it is your responsibility to create a functional workplace in which they can practice getting better.

11

Focusing Your Attention

Managers and leaders from every organization I have entered in recent years have told me that change is a pressing matter in their workplace. They speak of new technologies, converging markets, evolving consumers, and workforces that are being transformed. Much is spoken—and written—on predicting the direction of change. But there is more to this dilemma—an aspect that corporate trendsetters often shrug aside. It is deciding *where to focus your attention* as the change unfolds.

Obviously, the dysfunctional employees will need some attention. But what about your needs? As you've read through the preceding material, you may have recognized some dysfunctions of your own and want to know what to do about them. If so, then this chapter is for you. On the other hand, you could be questioning all this fuss about dysfunction. You could be thinking, "So I'm not fully functional; big deal. Neither is anyone else around here." Keep reading—this chapter is for you, too.

Uncovering dysfunction in the workplace is like locating termites in your house. You may suspect they're there because you've seen the signs, but you don't know where they are or how to get at them. If getting rid of them is your top priority, you will have to remove the floorboards and wall coverings to do the job right. On the other hand, you may be aware of the termites, but decide to put off treatment until you have more time and money. Meanwhile, the damage to the framework will continue, perhaps until the roof or floorboards collapse.

The workplace is another story. Frequently, you are able to determine the order in which you expose and address dysfunction. But not always. Sometimes events dictate a change in your priorities. Much as a house remodeling will expose termites, organizationwide undertakings such as quality improvement, team building, reinventing, or downsizing will flush out dysfunction. Something as innocent as a new phone system or a computer upgrade can shift your focus in a hurry. For example, you may not have planned to get involved in a simple office relocation, but there you are solving the problem of who will get the window office and deciding who will get the new desks and chairs. Whenever there is a lot more going on than you expected, you have probably uncovered some dysfunction. How about the time you tried to adjust the work schedule, and found yourself in meeting after meeting with upper management and the union rep? Remember when you suggested a cross-training program and "all hell broke loose"?

Large organizations are good places for dysfunction to hide. To find it, you have to focus on each separate work unit. In doing so, be alert for problems that are attributed to individual personalities. For example, a group of employees may candidly tell you that they are having problems with Mr. Teflon, and that if you got rid of him, things would get better. But when you try to focus on exactly what he has done to deserve their mistrust, none of their charges stick.

There really was a Mr. Teflon; like the coating on a frying pan, nothing stuck to him.

This nickname was once given to a manager who gave ambiguous directives that almost always needed clarification. If his subordinates got things right, he took the credit. But when things went awry, even though they had acted on the information he had given them, he denied ever having said such a thing. He frequently said things to one person off the record while sharing a slightly altered version of the same confidential information with another. When the two subordinates got together and compared confidences, they discovered Mr. Teflon's duplicity. When they shared their concerns with coworkers, they discovered that this was typical of how he turned people against each other.

I was working there on one occasion when this happened, and I was asked to confront the manager during a meeting with his subordinates. When he was presented with a list of names and specific statements, he acted surprised and denied saying anything. When everyone in the group disagreed and one after another repeated what they had been told, Mr. Teflon skillfully shifted the blame, declaring, "Well, I may have said it, but you should not have passed it on. I thought we had an agreement not to spread rumors. Even if I did say what you say I said, you had no right to pass it on." He then proceeded to chew them out for violating his confidence, and abruptly ended the session by declaring that he would no longer trust any of them. The group looked around at one another in dismay. They realized that despite their determined effort, none of their allegations had stuck to Mr. Teflon. After that experience, they completely lost their faith in him. The sad thing is, they also stopped trusting one another.

A change in senior management is less likely to stir up dysfunction than a change of supervisor or lead person. It seems that management changes at the higher levels have minimal influence on what happens at the working level. But while a change in department heads might go unnoticed, replacing a first-line supervisor can have a dramatic impact on production—and, consequently, on your management priorities.

Today's instantaneous electronic communication can also facilitate dysfunctional behaviors. As people rely less on face-to-face communication and more on electronic means, they pay less attention to traditional policies, standards, and procedures. Speed is often obtained at the expense of accuracy. In a dysfunctional workplace, electronic communications are highly susceptible to misinterpretation. Dysfunctional employees won't pause to seek clarification of an ambiguous message—and they think nothing of passing on the rumors and half-baked ideas that their coworkers send them as

E-mail. If you need to get a message across to your employees, remember that computer mail and telephone messages are poor substitutes for serious problem solving and legitimate decision making.

Facing the Challenge

The premise of this book is that mainstream methods don't work in a dysfunctional workplace. In this setting, you will need a different set of tools. In previous chapters, you have been introduced to a variety of tools and techniques designed for use in a dysfunctional workplace. I hope there is room in your box for one more. The model depicted in Figure 11-1 will help you to influence dysfunctional work behaviors in a positive way.

Imagine that you are conducting a team meeting. Some people want to solve a recurring workflow problem. Others

Figure 11-1. History and future model.

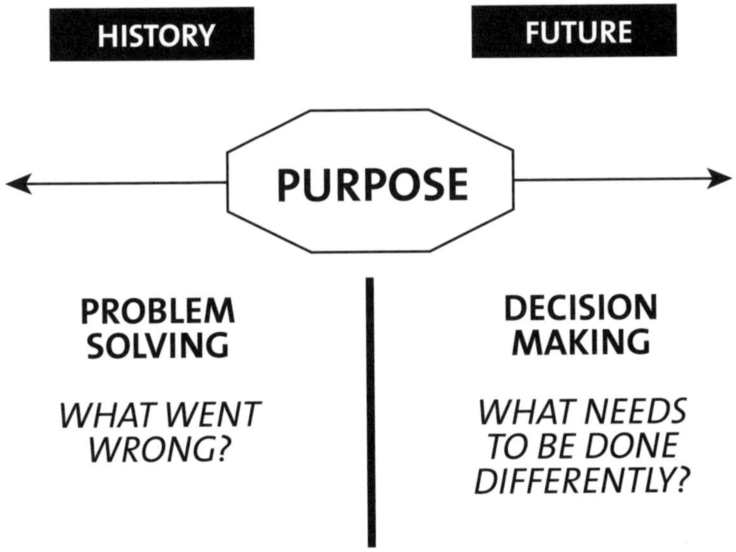

HISTORY

FUTURE

PURPOSE

PROBLEM SOLVING

WHAT WENT WRONG?

DECISION MAKING

WHAT NEEDS TO BE DONE DIFFERENTLY?

argue that the problem would resolve itself, were the production process changed. Both arguments have merit, and both need to be addressed. What would you do at this point? If you already have a way to handle this situation, set it aside for a moment while I describe how to use the history/future model shown in Figure 11-1.

Problem solving and decision making are two separate functions that demand different sets of skills and behaviors. If you try to perform both functions at the same time, you will find that it is not only very difficult and time-consuming, but energy-draining as well. The purpose of the history/future model is to isolate problem solving from decision making and provide you with a systematic way of working with both.

Problem Solving

When you look at the left side of the history/future model, you see that the focus question is, "What went wrong?" A problem exists when there is a difference between what was expected and what happened. Your purpose in problem solving is to look at history to find out the cause of the deviation and to develop a solution that will rectify that situation. To do this properly, you must put on your manager hat and call forth your managerial skills.

The following is a list of manager competencies that are measurable and therefore can be improved. As you review this list, think about which of these competencies you are comfortable with and which you need to develop further. Consider applying your strengths more frequently. Focus on what you do well and look at those in which you are less skillful as potential growth opportunities.

Judgment: The Ability To:

- Reach logical conclusions.
- Make high-quality choices based on available information.

* Identify pressing needs and set priorities.
* Critically evaluate written communications.

Organization: The Ability To:

* Plan, schedule, and control the work of others.
* Use resources sensibly.
* Deal with paperwork.
* Cope with multiple time demands.

Problem Analysis: The Ability To:

* Search for relevant data.
* Analyze complex information.
* Select the most significant elements.
* Identify and prioritize options.

Sensitivity: The Ability To:

* Perceive the needs, concerns, and problems of others.
* Work through conflicts by listening to both sides.
* Be tactful when dealing with persons of different backgrounds.
* Deal effectively with emotional issues.

Delegation: The Ability To:

* Assess the reliability and competence of subordinates.
* Reach clear conclusions on implementation strategies.
* Assign specific actions to the most appropriate persons.
* Define standards for evaluation and performance measurement.

Interpersonal: The Ability To:

* Listen and support the ideas of others.
* Give and receive constructive feedback.
* Share personal feelings and beliefs.
* Work productively in groups.

Political: The Ability To:

* Identify key issues involving formal and informal leaders.

- Use organizational policies to achieve goals.
- Establish cooperative relationships with key people.
- Realign power and form new coalitions.

Note: The list of selected skill dimensions presented above was taken in part from the University of California Management Assessment Center assessor's guide.

Making Decisions

As we shift our attention to the right side of the history/future model, you will see that the focus also shifts. The purpose question here is, "What needs to be done differently?" Making decisions is more about assessing future concerns and setting a new course of action to change what has happened in the past. You will be judged on your ability to initiate action that produces results. Put on your leader hat, as you will also be expected to assume leadership responsibilities.

In a five-year study of outstanding leaders, the well-known authority Warren Bennis and his coauthor, Burt Nanus, identified four competencies common to leaders. They determined that "the factor that empowers the workforce and ultimately determines which organizations succeed or fail is *leadership.*" Bennis and Nanus defined four leadership strategies or competencies that are evident to some extent in every one of the ninety leaders interviewed for their study:*

1. *Attention through vision.*
   - Communicate an extraordinary focus of commitment that attracts people.
   - Bring others to a place they have not been before.
   - Establish a set of intentions for the vision.
   - Create a sense of outcome, goal, or direction.
2. *Meaning through communication.*
   - Make the vision apparent to others.

*Warren Bennis and Burt Nanus, *Leaders: Strategies for Taking Charge* (New York: Harper & Row, 1985). Copyright © 1985 by Warren Bennis and Burt Nanus. Reprinted by permission of HarperCollins Publishers, Inc.

- Bring people into alignment around the vision.
- Clarify what the vision means to everyone.
- Communicate through organization layers, special interest groups, and opponents.

3. *Trust through positioning.*
   - Provides reliability and establishes constancy.
   - People know what the leader stands for.
   - Encourages open disagreement and discussion.
   - Holds to a firmly stated viewpoint.
4. *The development of self.*
   - Leaders know their own skills and deploy them effectively.
   - Leaders know themselves and use their strengths.
   - Leaders work on improving their weaknesses.
   - Leaders concentrate on the intention, the task, and the decision.

Management and leadership skills can be felt throughout the organization. They give pace and energy to the workplace. In functional organizations, this combination is most evident in four themes: (1) People feel significant; (2) learning and competence matter; (3) people are part of a community; and (4) work is exciting and meaningful.

Management of Meaning

The management of meaning was introduced earlier as a leadership competency. Let's take a moment here to expand that discussion and relate it to overcoming dysfunction in your workplace. Time and again I have asked you to reflect on the specific stages of organizational dysfunction. Bear with me as we go through them one more time.

At stage 1, vague directions create ambiguity, which, if not questioned, leads to multiple interpretations and inconsistent behaviors. If the inconsistencies are being ignored, the level of dysfunction has reached stage 2. When it becomes politically incorrect to point out the ambiguities and discuss the inconsistencies, the dysfunction has progressed to stage 3. At this stage, management is isolated from the truth and cannot see what is happening. Stage 4 is attained when management fails to address serious problems because no one will discuss them.

In a nutshell, when you are in a functional organization, you can always tell it like it is. People will know what you mean and act upon it because they know what it is. But in a dysfunctional workplace, people won't know what you mean by it. As the organization has progressed through stages 1, 2, and 3, it has meant different things to different people at different times. So, no matter how many ways you say it, they won't buy it because it has no meaning for them. Without meaning, your team will forfeit their collective understanding, acceptance, and perspective.

Attending to Your Needs

During the current period of *organizational unraveling,* with people moving up, moving down, and moving out, it is critical to your health and welfare that you have a personal support system. But those around you won't be useful for support if they are also caught up in dysfunction. A simple job change or career move doesn't always work, either. In fact, such actions are often accompanied by a struggle between self-support and reliance on others. As your organization and the people in it grapple with dysfunction, you must look to other sources to reaffirm your own relevance and purpose.

If you are like most of the managers I've worked with, your sense of purpose and value is drawn from the traditional employment relationship. In a dysfunctional workplace, relying on an organization-based support system to meet your needs is risky.

In his book *Healing the Wounds: Overcoming the Trauma of Layoffs and Revitalizing Downsized Organizations,* David Noer refers to the concept of having all of one's needs met by the organization as the "taproot strategy." Noer poses several thought-provoking questions, including, "What happens if the taproot gets cut? If who you are is where you work, what are you if you lose your job?'' Organizationally dependent people, he says, ''rely on an employer to nurture all aspects of their life. Their self-esteem, identity, and social worth are nourished by a single organization.'' When they are released from their jobs, these people see no meaning to their lives.*

Another thing to bear in mind: As you change, your support system must change also. People in your current support system, if you have one, support you because they like who and what you are right now—they may not want you to change. In fact, they'll frequently work against you if you try to change. So, how do you get the support you need if you can no longer count on people in the workplace? You build your own support system—one that meets your needs.

Functions and Players

Your support system is made up of all the ''supporting players'' in your life. Assembling them takes time and requires a great deal of thought. Think of it as a series of ''casting calls.'' People audition, and you carefully consider who would be the best person to play each part. The process of selection is not done in secret. It works best if you let people know what role you would like them to assume and, should they agree, what you expect them to do when you call on them for support.

Unlike the case with mentoring or networking, your support system will focus on you as a person, rather than on your job or career. The primary mode of communication between yourself and the role players in your system should be one-on-one. At times, the level of interaction can be intense, particularly during periods of change. Often, when you aren't sure what's really bugging you, exploring the deeper aspects of problems with someone in your support system will bring the

*David M. Noer, *Healing the Wounds: Overcoming the Trauma of Layoffs and Revitalizing Downsized Organizations* (San Francisco: Jossey-Bass, Inc. Publishers, 1995). Reprinted with permission. Copyright © 1995 Jossey-Bass, Inc., Publishers, 350 Sansome Street, San Francisco, CA 94104 (800)-956-7739.

issue to the surface so that you can face it honestly. This is particularly helpful when you're working to overcome your own dysfunctions.

The following descriptions of support system roles have been developed from the research and writings of pioneers in the career development field. The six roles presented here have been selected to fit the needs of managers who are struggling with dysfunction in their workplace.

1. *Confidence builder.* The key function of a confidence builder is to provide encouragement when you need a lift. Choose people who respect you for who you are, not for what you do. People who know you well are better able to sense when your spirits need a boost. Most managers rely on their own self-confidence to get them through the rough spots. However, when the rough spots turn into tough times, it's comforting to know people who can supply you with the assurance you need to get back on track.

2. *Challenger.* This role requires someone who will question your flight plan if he or she thinks you need a course correction. You frequently need a sturdy sounding board to test your notions, thoughts, and ideas. The stronger your convictions are, the more people you need in this role. Finding people who will say no, if no really is the best answer, is not an easy assignment. Just as you demand much of yourself, so must you demand much from the challengers in your support systems. You will place demands on their time to listen to you, on their intellect to take you seriously, and on their willpower to refute your assumptions.

3. *Motivator.* Managers need relationships with people who stimulate their thinking and prompt them when they need a reality check. These people are like a starter on an engine—particularly useful when, after a period of idleness, you need a quick burst of energy to get moving again. Pick people who inspire you and build you up. They don't have to know you to be helpful. Authors, artists, poets, preachers, prophets, gurus, or just about anyone who provides a positive influence qualifies as a motivator.

4. *Sustainer.* The sustainer is concerned for your welfare and your well-being. Just like the body, the mind needs nourishment if it is to grow and develop. When your mental health sags, you need someone who will not just prop you up, but lift you up. You need to know that there are people who care what happens to you. Helping you to look for opportunity in adversity is one way in which players in this role can help you broaden and develop your horizons.

5. *Friend.* Friends are people who care for you and admire the way you are. They think you're a special person, and they don't try to change you. You can trust them to respect your point of view, even if they disagree with it. They openly discuss their personal concerns and easily express their frank opinions. Spending time with friends provides a type of stimulation that is rarely found in a dysfunctional workplace.

6. *Reflector.* These are people who think like you, have the same interests as you, and agree with you on important issues. Because they are like you in many ways and value many of the same things you do, they serve as a "mirror" reflecting your thoughts and feelings. You are comfortable bouncing ideas around in their presence without fear of judgment or criticism. They accept your faults and forgive your mistakes.

Noted career development authority Beverly Kaye recommends limiting the number of support roles you assign to any one person. The convenience of going to a single source for a variety of support needs is overshadowed by the possibility of stressing out that special person by expecting him or her to wear too many hats.

If the place you work becomes more complex or the dysfunction deepens, you may need to look outside the organization for people to fill some of the roles. Finding people who are willing to provide the support you need is difficult. I strongly encourage you to take the time to develop at least a partial list of candidates when you finish this chapter. The time you invest in building a support system can provide you with a great source of independent strength as you strive to overcome the dysfunction in your workplace.

12

Communicating Intent

Years ago, at a workshop on communication, the trainer handed out a list of what he called "Power Points in Listening." Although each point was relevant, two struck me as being the most significant:

1. You cannot *not* communicate.
2. Whenever contact is made, communication occurs.

These statements have helped me understand that *communicating intent* involves a lot more than just conveying words. When words are transferred from one person to another, their *intention* may not be fully understood by either. Studies on listening have shown that even when a message is perceived, 70 to 90 percent of it is lost or changed in the transmission.

What is involved in communicating intent? On an individual level, it requires you to *say what you mean, and mean what you say.* On the organizational level, you must *confirm that what you said or heard aligns with what was meant* (preferably before any action is taken).

Functional employees have no trouble realizing when management's intentions are not clear. They know because they sense a lack of perspective, understanding, and acceptance. When this occurs, they find out what they need to know or locate reliable sources for information. Dysfunctional employees also sense that something isn't right, but instead of searching for the true meaning behind an unclear directive, they simply whine and complain that no one ever tells them anything.

If you pay attention to the communication channels in your organization, you may find this dysfunction at work. In a dysfunctional organization, communication going down the chain of command is directive, authoritative, and task-focused. Coming back up, it takes the form of complaining, criticism, and resistance.

I once overheard a disgruntled employee in the break room complaining that his boss had a plan all right, but only shared it with the "brownnosers" who hung around his office after work. This unhappy chap declared that he would not kiss anybody's backside just to find out what was happening. His bluster was rewarded with a round of cheers and slaps on the back from those near enough to reach him.

Later that day, I had an opportunity to meet with many of these same folks. After letting them know what I'd overheard in the break room, I challenged them to tell me how keeping information from them would benefit their boss. Following several halfhearted attempts to respond, the fellow I had overheard in the break room suggested that there might not be any good reason, other than the fact that their boss was a jerk. When the laughter subsided, I acknowledged that possibility, but challenged them to tell me why working for a jerk should prevent them from doing a good job. They soon understood that their boss was not intentionally hiding information from them; he just didn't know how to communicate. We spent the remainder of that day defining ways in which they could seek clarification from their boss whenever they were not clear about his intentions.

Building Relationships

There is little trust in a dysfunctional workplace. Employees are usually forced to build working relationships before they are given the opportunity to learn to trust one another. The widespread adoption of electronic messaging (E-mail) has further reduced the amount of face-to-face communication between all levels of employees, making the development of trust even less likely.

Why? Many managers rely on E-mail or other memorandum formats to ensure that they are communicating the same message in exactly the same words to all recipients. Dysfunctional employees prefer this, because they find this level of communication less threatening than a typical meeting. But E-mail and memorandums actually increase the likelihood of misunderstanding because they are highly subject to ambiguity.

How many times have you been frustrated by a meeting with several employees in which each waves a copy of your latest directive, quotes what you said, notes what you *obviously* meant, and then offers a different interpretation? Without the support of a truthful dialogue, nonverbal communications are subject to individual interpretation and thus are primary sources of ambiguity and inconsistency. Remember, in a dysfunctional system, it is difficult to clarify your intention unless you have the opportunity to align your verbal and nonverbal communications.

What's Missing

It's frustrating when the outcome of a directive differs radically from what you intended. In a functional setting, you're likely to have found out about the unintended consequences *before* they happened. Those around you would have realized that you are only human—like them—and given you a chance to correct any misunderstanding. But what if you are in a dysfunctional workplace? Confusion and finger-pointing are the usual results. The enormous potential for waste of such a communications calamity is perfectly illustrated by the following true story:

Picture a small city, population 15,000, run by a city manager serving at the discretion of an elected city council. According to the local newspaper, expenditures were getting out of hand, and the council was under pressure to monitor the budget more closely. Adding fuel to the fire was adverse community reaction to a recent round of pay raises for the city manager and department heads. The current administrator had every reason to be worried about his job: The city had a history of strife between the council and a succession of short-lived city managers.

In an effort to overcome its own poor history, the council brought in a consultant—me—to improve organizational communications and teamwork, and to help forge stronger ties between the council members and their city management team. To get the ball rolling, I was invited to sit in on a closed-door personnel meeting in which the council assessed each department head.

At the meeting, the city manager was under pressure to justify the salaries of his department heads. After discussing various options, including the freezing of all salaries, the council recommended that department heads get out into the community more, to let the voters see who runs the city.

After the city manager passed on that recommendation to the department heads, the public works director and the superintendent spent the next day driving around the city. The following morning, the superintendent met with the garbage crews as they were warming up their trucks and told them that instead of collecting garbage, they would be trimming mistletoe from all the trees in the park. Garbage collection would have to wait.

Next morning the city hall switchboard lit up with complaints about garbage left sitting. The city manager and the public works director tracked down the superintendent, who was surprised by their concern. He explained that during their drive around the city, the public works director had told him that the council wanted some action to justify department salaries. However, since the only specific thing the director had commented on during their trip was the overgrowth of the mistletoe, the superintendent assumed it to be a priority.

The city council, in a mood to fire everyone connected with the fiasco, called an emergency meeting, which I was also asked to attend. I sat patiently as the council recited story after story of previous incidents involving the public works department. Finally, everyone took a breath and turned to me. By then I had more than enough ammunition to show them how their organizational dysfunction had contributed to all these unintended consequences. Slowly, the council's attitude shifted from retribution to reconciliation. By the time the meeting ended, so had everyone's desire for finger-pointing. They were ready for a change.

Unintended Consequences

The challenge in the mistletoe case was one you may frequently face as a manager: what issues to address first. Even if the organizational, individual, and group problems are evident and the collective intention is clearly to overcome dysfunction, there is often no clear place to start.

Unless someone or something is begging for your attention, you may have to start by making a list of *unintended consequences.* It helps if you take off your "hat of responsibility" when you do this. That means that you set aside your positional authority and just be *yourself* while you contemplate a few instances or incidents where the outcome wasn't what you intended. That outcome doesn't have to have been negative, by the way—you can learn a lot from an unintended positive outcome, especially if you want to replicate it. Finally, it helps to write these in a brief story format. The following examples of actual cases are offered here to get you started.

* In an effort to boost morale, management decided to form a company baseball team. The person assigned to order equipment was unfamiliar with the game. He correctly assumed that most players were right-handed, but wrongly concluded that they would catch the ball with a glove worn on that hand. The team was surprised when they were issued left-handed mitts.

* A produce clerk who was unfamiliar with the avocado and uncertain what "perishable" meant stored a newly arrived shipment in the freezer. Responding to the newspaper ad touting the many qualities of this delicious fruit, customers quickly bought out the lot. Just as quickly, they angrily returned it, disgusted by the blackened pulp they had discovered when they sliced through the skin.

* A newly installed computer payroll system incorrectly treated a year-end Christmas bonus as a pay raise. This error pushed most employees into a higher tax bracket, triggering an automatic deduction of back taxes for the entire year from the next paycheck. Employees were astounded to have re-

ceived $0.00 pay because the amount deducted was more than their bimonthly earnings. The direct deposit system was also thrown into chaos because it couldn't cope with zero as an amount.

As you ponder your list of unintended consequences in your company, revisit the dysfunctional behaviors checklist (Chapter 1) to see which items might readily apply. For example, if you checked any of the following items, there's probably not much inclusionary thinking going on in your organization:

- ❑ Isolation keeps management from seeing what is happening.
- ❑ Management isolation is used as the basis of decision making by cliques.
- ❑ Gossip is used to excite and titillate.
- ❑ Secrets are used to build alliances.

Creating Openness

Trust is essential to any functional relationship. In order to transform a dysfunctional relationship to a functional one, you must be honest in your communications with one another and learn to trust one another. This is not always easy. Your intention in communicating honestly is to achieve clarity and understanding, not to hurt people's feelings. However, that may happen anyway—especially when you're dealing with a dysfunctional person.

Let's say you receive a report from an employee that isn't what you asked for. From past experience, you know that this employee doesn't handle criticism well and gets upset easily when challenged. You don't want to make him feel bad; you just want him to do a better job. You need this information for your presentation, and you cannot use what he's turned in.

What do you do? Well, you could be straightforward with

your concerns, or you could select one of many feedback methods designed to soften the emotional impact. I guarantee that the latter approach works better. Truth telling is an admirable quality, but it is not one that is valued by a dysfunctional employee. Still, crafting your statements so that they carry no blame or judgment takes practice. If you're not used to being open and direct, it might help if you "script" your message. The following is an example of a scripted message that can be communicated either in person or in writing:

"My intent in sharing this with you is to build our relationship and to help you understand what I need in the future, not to make you feel bad. I recognize that what I say may hurt your feelings, but I'm hopeful that that feeling won't last. I'm confident that our relationship will eventually reach a level where I don't have to choose my words carefully to avoid hurt feelings. The sole intention of this communication is to clarify my expectations so that in the future we both get what we want."

While language such as this may seem awkward at first, that's okay. The fact that it is "not like you" shows the recipient that you are willing to try something new. It also will be evident that you want to change the way things are—a crucial first step in building relationships with those who report to you. What about those at your level and above?

When communicating your intent is not the issue, and understanding the intent of others is, you may have to adjust the content of your message. For instance, in seeking clarification from your superiors, especially if their functionality is suspect, you'll want to avoid implying that they are poor communicators. In addition, when reaching up the chain of command, take care not to suggest culpability in your message. Until you've developed a repertoire of your own, feel free to borrow from the following short list of phrases:

I don't know where I stand with you.
This way of communicating doesn't work for me.
I'm really excited about this task, but I need more (time, information, etc.) to do it the way you require.
I'm disappointed with these results because I had higher expectations.

I'm not happy right now and need time to think about my response.

Finding the right way to challenge the intentions of your peers is difficult, but certainly possible. The content of your message is less important than the approach you take. So the trick is to choose the right path.

This concept may be easier to grasp if you think about it in terms of family life. As a kid, I could usually tell how my parents related to visitors by the way the visitors entered the house. A knock on the back door meant neighbors and was greeted with smiles and shouts of, "Come on in, the door's open." A ring of the front doorbell could herald the arrival of formal company or a stranger, and thus evoked a more cautious response.

Your approach to peers might follow one of the following paths, depending upon your appreciation and awareness of their receptivity and functionality:

- *Sympathy.* A sympathetic approach implies a readiness to agree and indicates that you are seeking mutual understanding. Use it with functional people in situations where you truly want to understand their intentions and are willing to acknowledge their feelings, even though you may disagree with their perspective once you understand it. The sympathetic approach is not as useful with dysfunctional people. They are less likely to understand their own feelings and will therefore find it difficult to discuss them. All is not lost, however. A sympathetic dialogue could afford them a rare opportunity to have their feelings acknowledged without being the focus of blame. It could lay the groundwork for use of this path in the future.
- *Empathy.* An empathic approach gives you the option of connecting on either an intellectual or an emotional level. It shows that you have insights to share and are seeking a deeper exploration of the issues. This path is a good one to take with functional colleagues who are interested in developing closer ties. It does require more time and frequent con-

nections, but the potential payoff makes that worthwhile. Empathy also works with dysfunctional peers, but only up to a point. Their willingness to communicate with you is likely to stop once it's clear that you understand and accept their intentions. When they are satisfied they have gotten their position across, they will become disinclined to go any further. You're liable to find that your communication is strictly one-way from then on. If that happens, and you still wish to make your intentions known, try the next approach.

* *Apathy.* Less comfortable than the other options, the apathetic approach works best with people who have demonstrated that they care more about their own feelings than about yours. That being the case, you might as well make your intentions known without regard to feelings. The apathetic approach is devoid of emotion. Using it demonstrates that you are interested only in results. This matter-of-fact approach cuts through the facade of pleasantry and communicates your intentions clearly. In most cases, this approach is reserved for dysfunctional peers who don't—or won't—respond to gentler communication styles. It demonstrates that all you want from the other party is confirmation of his or her intention and an understanding that you'll be back if the misunderstanding persists.

Empathy and sympathy are both useful pathways to people who lean toward functionality. In dealing with dysfunctional colleagues, however, apathy tends to work best. Once you establish truthful dialogue, you still have the challenge of communicating intent.

Inclusionary Thinking

One way to help develop the ability to communicate intent is through use of the following training technique. Look at the elements in the inclusionary thinking model, as shown in Figure 12-1. The model depicts the basic elements involved in communicating or clarifying intention. Five elements are shown, although additional elements can be added or substi-

Figure 12-1. Inclusionary thinking model.

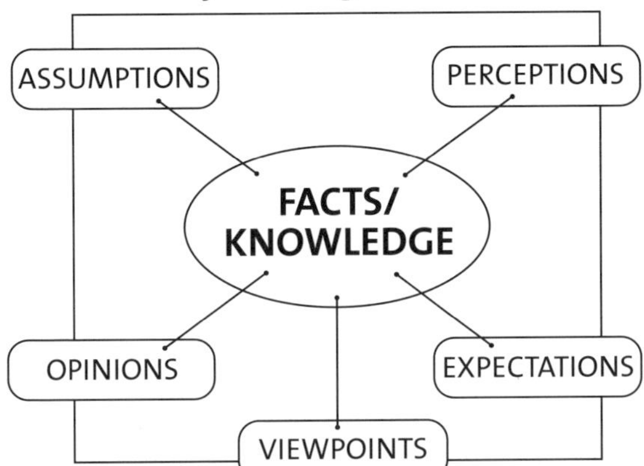

tuted, depending on your objective: resolving conflict, solving problems, making decisions, gathering information, developing plans, building community, or reaching consensus. This activity can be conducted verbally if everyone is comfortable with an open forum, or through note gathering if the risk of disclosure is too high.

Sharing "facts and knowledge" is the opening piece and central to the process. We can refer to it as "stirring the pot." The purpose of this first step is to uncover everything that is known about a specific situation by everyone involved in it. That would include all the outlying items in Figure 12-1: opinions, perceptions, viewpoints, assumptions, and expectations. As the process unfolds, you'll be amazed to discover how much of what you intended to communicate got through intact—and how much got lost along the way. It's important that you withhold or suspend judgment until you've finished stirring the pot. No one will value what you have to say until the things that the other people involved know have been completely digested, so you might as well keep your two cents in your pocket until then.

After helping your employees work their way through this process a few times, encourage them to try it on their own. Let them know that you'll be available to join the process if it should bog down, but you'd prefer to wait until they've finished stirring the pot and are ready to add new ingredients to the mix. They may not be successful at first, but eventually they will come to understand your intentions on their own.

You may recall from your earlier reading that dysfunctional employees don't trust the group process. This is particularly relevant when the topic is contentious and liable to pit one group against another. If that's your situation, you might consider using a nonverbal method developed by Dean Paulson of Organization Advocates. His version is called *The Truth as You Know It.* Participants anonymously write on 3 x 5 cards those issues that they would like to see resolved but aren't comfortable bringing up to the group. These are gathered together by the facilitator, who lists them on a flip chart one at a time. Paulson finds that this nonverbal method is useful when a group neither enjoys an environment that encourages dialogue nor understands the value of it. Paulson's exercise is designed "to make the point that listening, and a learning dialogue, will develop a fuller understanding and a more accurate point of view."

Any formally guided discussion exposes people, perhaps for the first time, to the possibility that they may not "know the truth," and that they may not be able to discover the truth on their own. According to Paulson, "These discussions usually evolve to a concurrence that no one possesses the absolute truth about anything and that judgment or conclusions are best made following the evaluation of all the data available on a given 'truth.' Even then a conclusion could be flawed."

The key to a successful experience with the inclusionary thinking model is to pose the right questions. It helps if you know what questions you want answered. Expect the participants to add questions as the available facts and knowledge unfold.

* *Assumptions:* What conclusions have people brought with them? What do they actually know? What information is missing? How open are they? Do their assumptions differ? How accurate were they in making their assumptions?
* *Opinions:* What do people believe? What do they think should happen? Who has taken a stand? Who is open to

change? Are people proactive or reactive? How were their opinions drawn?

* *Perceptions:* What do people think has happened? What information has gotten through? What needs correcting? How clear is everyone? Who is aware and who is not?
* *Expectations:* What are the anticipated outcomes? Are people working from the Dis-List (see Figure 7-2)? If so, what happened? Have they relied on internal or external sources for their information? How are they measuring the response? Are they thinking about the past, present, or future? What's the difference between what they wanted and what they got?
* *Viewpoints:* What do people see from where they sit? What organizational positions are represented? Are they looking at the facts from above, below, or across? Whose views are blocked, and by what?

Developing Inclusionary Thinking

> Having lived long, I have experienced many instances of being obliged by better information, or fuller consideration, to change opinions even on important subjects, which I once thought right, but found to be otherwise. It is therefore that the older I grow, the more apt I am to doubt my own judgment, and to pay more respect to the judgment of others. (Ben Franklin, 1787)

The wisdom of Ben Franklin is more applicable today than it was two hundred years ago. Inclusionary thinkers, like Ben, seek out and consider all views before making a decision. The benefits of inclusionary thinking can be demonstrated by forming a small group of people into a tight circle. Mark an X on one side of a paper cup and place it in the middle of the circle. Ask for a show of hands of those who *cannot* see an X from where they sit. Point out that if the X represented an important fact, many of them would have missed it. This exercise demonstrates the importance of valuing other points of view and sharing yours, especially when there is a difference. In a training exercise, it's easy to move people around so that they can see the X or to rotate the cup so that the X is visible, because the people involved are all in the same room at the same time. But when folks are spread throughout the organization and deal with each other and the issues only in meetings, the communication process is the only method of transmitting intent.

Dysfunctional organizations don't support inclusionary thinking. Formal lines of authority are vertical and therefore flow from positions of power down to the less powerful. As information moves downward, people at various levels assess its contents and consequences on the basis of how it affects them. Informal communications tend to follow informal (personal) relationship lines as individuals share their interpretations in the hallway, cafeteria, or parking lot.

The tone and tenor of communications in a dysfunctional organization are likely to be exclusionary, that is, designed to keep others from knowing. Dysfunctional people are particularly keen on keeping information away from those in authority. From their perspective, management isolation is not only purposeful, but necessary for survival. Why?

Remember the section on school-family systems in Chapter 4, where we addressed the ways in which individuals are influenced by others when they are placed in a social system, such as the workplace? In turn, these various social systems dictate the conditions for acceptance and socialization. Most often, they do it in a negatively directed manner. In other words, for the sake of the collective good, authority figures such as teachers, parents, and bosses teach children, students, and subordinates what *not* to do.

This is one of the reasons that dysfunctional employees have difficulty understanding their purpose in an organizational setting. While they may have a clear understanding of what they are *not* to do, most of them have never been taught how to set personal goals, let alone how to tie them to organizational objectives. In order to stay out of trouble, they focus more on their boss than on themselves, and strive to produce what they think their boss wants. Even when their opinions are sought, dysfunctional employees usually dissemble, and say only what they think the boss wants to hear. (This is one reason organizationwide surveys tend to be unreliable.)

Consider for a moment how often teaching and training are negatively directed. When I ask people in training sessions to tell me why they are attending, they most often answer that:

I was just told to be here.
I dunno. I guess I did something wrong.

Think about some of the places you've worked. Which did you spend more time on, giving recognition or counseling poor performers? Which did you spend more energy on, handing out rewards or doling out discipline? Think back over your own career. What do you remember more vividly, accolades or criticism? When children get their test papers back from the teacher, do the bright red checks draw their attention to their errors or to the questions they answered correctly? The sole purpose of many of our testing processes is to catch mistakes and teach us to avoid them in the future—to teach us what *not* to do. It's no wonder employees want to maintain a cloak of invisibility from their employers. Your challenge, then, is to overcome that basic instinct.

Mistletoe Revisited

For a demonstration of how the inclusionary thinking model works, return with me now to the mistletoe scenario outlined earlier in this chapter.

When all the players assembled in the council chamber the following day, we worked through the inclusionary thinking model, step by step. As the story unfolded, it became clear that the council members knew nothing about the mistletoe trimming and we were stunned to learn that their well-intentioned directive (to "get out in the public more") had inadvertently halted the garbage pickup.

All they had intended was for the department heads to have higher community visibility, and not sit in their offices all day. They envisioned appearances at Chamber of Commerce functions, speeches to the downtown association, presentations to the service clubs, and interviews on local TV and radio stations. In other words, the council expected the department heads to mingle with the citizens and promote the council's vision of the city's future.

The city manager perceived their directive differently. He thought that the council was upset with his "overpaid" department heads for not earning their keep. His strategy was to light a fire under them before he lost his job. The public works director, in turn, viewed the request as additional work for him. If there were infrastructure problems somewhere in the city, he'd better find them quickly and set about fixing them. After all, he was close to retirement and didn't want anything to mess that up. The superintendent simply thought that the director was mad at him for something. This made him very uncomfortable and eager to get back on his boss's good side by attending to whatever was bugging him. The crew knew that something was screwy, but they kept their opinions to themselves and did what they were told without question.

As each of the players added his or her views, assumptions, perceptions, expectations, and opinions to the newly formed body of knowledge, they all began to see, perhaps for the first time, that they were dysfunctional. At first they were disappointed and disillusioned by the discovery. But, with a little push, they revisited some of their past misadventures. The trip was worthwhile, for it made them realize just how poorly they had been communicating their intentions from one level to the next. The council members agreed to work with the city manager and the department heads to find better ways of communicating their intentions.

Soon thereafter, encouraged by their ability to improve communication, the management team developed a list of organizational dysfunctions and set about overcoming them all. It didn't take long for the supervisors and staff to get on board. Gradually, as other citizens were drawn into the process of assessing the level of services and recommending changes, the atmosphere of tension and suspicion was replaced by one of anticipation and cooperation. All small cities and towns struggle to match budget limitations with citizens' expectations for quality services, but this city learned how to make that struggle pay off, once everyone involved learned how to communicate intent effectively.

13

Achieving Purpose

When an organization engages me to assess its level of dysfunction, my initial intention is to discover its purpose. Once that is clearly understood, I can assess how well that purpose has been achieved and, if necessary, help realign those processes that are not serving the organization well. Given the choice, I prefer to meet first with the folks who "touch it and feel it" every day. After more than thirty years of poking around inside hundreds of organizations (large and small), I've come to appreciate that a functional organization's purpose must be clearly evident at every level, not just the top. In a dysfunctional organization, the purpose may be known at the top but not practiced at the point closest to the customer, or vice versa. If this ambiguous condition continues undiscovered, it can lead to inconsistencies that impede the organization's purpose.

Your best chance to lessen the impact of dysfunction in your workplace is to catch it at the earliest possible stage. Stage 1, you may recall, is where ambiguity is not questioned. If you don't catch it here, then it will progress to stage 2, where inconsistencies are ignored. At these early stages, the key to overcoming dysfunction is to uncover the ambiguity and provide clarification before the inconsistencies develop.

The trick is to get the employees involved in the search for ambiguity so that your customers or clients never experience inconsistency.

Ambiguity is not hard to uncover if you know where to look. How many companies do you know that toss out buzzwords like *product quality, service excellence,* and *customer focus,* then disempower their employees when the customer shows up? Take your bank, for example. When you enter the lobby with a complicated problem, you are at the point furthest from the person who can do you the most good. The nearest employee is a teller, who is limited to accepting deposits and cashing checks. If your service needs are complex, you're passed along to a supervisor, who dutifully explains why what you want is against corporate policy. Policy exceptions, it seems, are handled by the manager—who is out for the day at a customer service seminar.

Uncovering Ambiguity

The above example may overstate the point, but it does raise one critical question: What is the purpose of a bank? Is it to improve the financial position of the depositors or that of the stockholders? The answer is, both. Banking, like many other industries, is fraught with ambiguity. When employees appear to the customer to be incompetent, the reality frequently is that they don't understand their purpose—or if they do, they lack the power to pursue it.

Banks aren't alone in that regard. According to *Fortune* magazine's "The 1998 American Customer Satisfaction Index," aggregate scores for personal computer manufacturers have fallen 10 percent in the past four years. As the writer noted, "Sure, the machines are more powerful than ever, but what good are they if you can't get through to the help lines?" It's hard to find a computer user who doesn't have a helpline story to tell. Two examples follow. As you read the two contrasting stories, pay attention to how ambiguity was handled.

The owner of a small business was loading some new software when her computer crashed. She tried everything suggested in the manual, but nothing worked. Reluctantly, she telephoned the free twenty-four-hour customer service help line. After twelve minutes on hold, she made contact with a human, who quickly shuffled her to the tech support line, where she was put on hold again. Forty-five minutes later, a tech support agent came on the line. Unable to diagnose the problem, he told her to insert the master file and restore the operating system.

Halfway through, the restore process stalled and the computer locked up again. It turned out the master disk was corrupted. The tech support agent offered to send a free replacement . . . if she would pay for shipping and handling. Even then, there was a hitch. Because it was after normal working hours, the disk wouldn't go out until the following day. She could expect her replacement to cover the 170-mile distance within five to ten working days.

Not wanting to wait that long, she requested overnight shipment and was stunned to hear, "We don't offer express shipping—only regular mail." Not believing that this major computer manufacturer would have such a stupid policy, she asked to speak to a manager and was told that "they were all in a meeting."

Undeterred, she offered to pay for overnight express using her own account. The tech support agent put her on hold to check, and then came back. "Sorry," he said, cheerfully, "we can't do that."

His final offer was to ship it priority mail—it would arrive within three to five days, with no guarantee of arrival date. Five days passed—no disk. She called the company's shipping department and discovered that the disk had been shipped by regular mail. It finally arrived two days later, having kept her out of business for a total of seven days—truly an unsatisfactory resolution.

That won't be the end of the story, however. She needed the new software because her business was growing. She also had plans to purchase a new computer system. When she goes shopping, there'll be no ambiguity in her mind about what *not* to buy.

Our second situation involved a similar set of circumstances with a different computer maker, but it ended happily for both the customer and the company.

In this case, the computer was a laptop owned by the CEO of a large health-care system. The machine wouldn't load a new software program, so he called the manufacturer's (800) help line. The telephone was answered promptly by a cheerful individual who thoughtfully took note of the problem. Then, instead of simply passing the customer to someone else, the spokesperson stayed on the line and dialed into additional departments as the customer listened. Tech support came on the line first to diagnose the problem and provide a solution. Next up was a service person to confirm software compatibility. Shipping joined the conference to arrange overnight delivery. Finally, a sales rep came on line with a product information update and current upgrade options. The next afternoon a replacement disk arrived—along with $500 worth of new software that the happy CEO had ordered while on the line.

Is there any doubt as to which of the above companies is achieving its purpose?

Lead, Follow, or Step Out of the Way

It has been my experience that a lot of companies direct the bulk of their leadership training efforts at the top and middle management levels. When it comes time for the line staff to attend, the money is running low, so the company sends a handful of employees to a train-the-trainer session. In turn, they're expected to pass on what they learn to the rest of the troops. Even if the instruction is good and the materials relevant, the programs seldom stay in place long enough to make a difference. Organizationwide programs take so long to implement that they're likely to be abandoned before everyone is included or replaced when something perceived as being better comes along.

You may be working for one of those companies that spends hundreds of thousands of dollars and several years certifying all the managers in the use of a hot-selling leadership program, only to have it scrapped when the CEO departs for greener pastures or finds another quick-fix program that looks better.

These top-down training efforts are referred to irreverently on the shop floor as "management by best-seller." The folks on the floor stay around longer than those at the top, and after a few years they tend to get cynical about attending the "program du jour." Too frequently these days I'm faced with a band of malcontents, arms folded tightly across their chests, chanting, "We've seen 'em come and we've seen 'em go, and this too shall pass"—referring, of course, to the training program I'm there to implement.

Sadly, an enormous amount of time, talent, and treasure are being wasted on one-size-fits-all training programs that focus on personality rather than purpose. Regardless of how management is defined or what the role of a leader might be, the achievement of purpose should be the ultimate objective. The theory you apply, in my view, is less significant than your ability to get people moving in the right direction.

So what does this mean to you? For starters, if you want to overcome the dysfunction in your workplace, you may have to alter the way you think, beginning with the assumption that leadership is positional and therefore is found mostly at the highest levels. Another defective assumption you may have to let go of is that to lead, you must be visible up front. Not so—this might have been true at one time, but not anymore. In fact, sometimes it's better to lead from behind so that you can see if everyone is headed in the right direction.

We tend to assume that a leader is someone who makes things happen. Leaders also stop things from happening—which is the basis for most consumer complaints. In today's customer-focused marketplace, initiating corrections, making adjustments, and authorizing refunds are all leadership activities.

Harry Truman made history with his famous line, "The buck stops here." He was not referring to money, of course, but to his leadership responsibility. But what worked in Harry's time won't work now. Things happen so fast that there is no time for the "buck" to work its way up to Harry's level. To succeed in a global marketplace, functional companies need responsible leaders at all levels who can act on the company's behalf at any time, day or night.

Leadership works best when it's informal and natural. Leadership skills can be acquired on the job with practice. Most people come by them naturally; all they need is the opportunity to apply them. Besides, you don't have time to officially appoint and formally train leaders. Finally, it's time we focused less on the personality of a leader and more on the process of leadership.

Figure 13-1 contains a summary of competencies listed by function. As you review each list, try to focus on the activity rather than the position. The list on the left represents those activities necessary to manage a situation. You can assign people to perform these functions based on their role in the organization and their knowledge of the past rather than their title or position. The information and expertise housed in the minds and hearts of your staff can be brought to bear on the situation quickly. They'll soon realize that it doesn't matter who the manager is, what counts is that the function is performed.

The same goes for the list on the right. These competencies are necessary if leadership is to occur; therefore, whoever performs them is the leader. As the old saying goes, "If it walks like a duck, quacks like a duck, and acts like a duck, then it must be a duck." Substitute "leader" for "duck" and you've got the picture. Again, who does it is not as important as getting it done.

You don't have to send people to a formal training program to learn these functions. Just ensure that they are clear on the organization's purpose before they assume either role.

Figure 13-1. History vs. future: leader competencies.

The beauty of this model is that once the issues have been identified and the purpose is known, the manager and leader functions can be performed by just about anyone.

Sometimes we make too big a deal of management and leadership development. They've gotten far more complex and time-consuming than necessary (not to mention expensive!). So, if you're looking for an easier way to get the job done, this model should serve your purpose well.

The models depicted in Figure 13-1 and its companion, Figure 13-2, are designed for use on the job rather than in a formal training session. Both work best when the people assigned to resolve the issue(s) are brought together. These models can also be used as a one-on-one coaching tool.

For now, let's focus on Figure 13-2. Start with a quick assessment—a simple show of hands will do. Ask the members of your team to think about the issue or situation at hand that's on the table and indicate whether they are "thinking back" or "thinking ahead." Then ask them to take a position on the side of the room that reflects their current mode of thinking. For example, seat those who are thinking ahead on the right and ask them to listen as those on the left reflect on the issue(s).

Remember, this is a process, not a procedure. It works best if you let it unfold in the most natural way possible. It also helps if the players are familiar with the group acceptance

Figure 13-2. History vs. future: key questions.

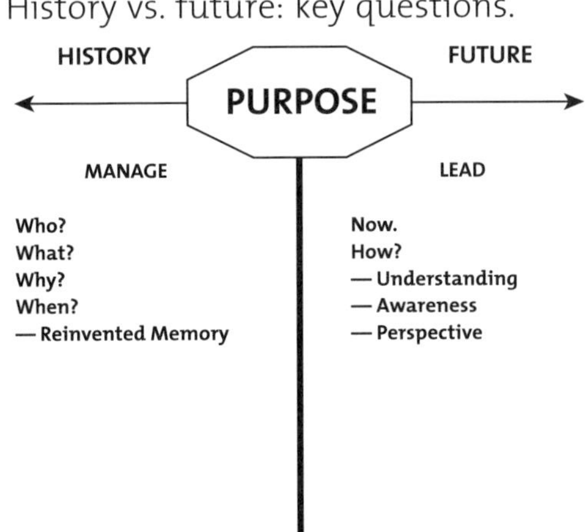

pact (Chapter 2). Determine before you start how much time you wish to spend on each side of the model. Encourage participants to change sides or take a new position if their focus changes. Ask people to withhold their comments and contributions unless they're sitting with the side that has the floor.

Using the key words shown in the "Manage" column, form a list of questions that are relevant to the situation. Keep the questions short and simple, like these:

1. ***Team Performance or Productivity***

* Who are we?
* Why are we here?
* What is our problem?
* When does this happen?

2. ***Customer Satisfaction or Service***

* Who filed the complaint?
* Why is this customer upset?
* What does this customer want?
* When does this customer need it?

Once the focus questions have been compiled, the data collection and confirmation can begin. It won't take long before the group's memory of the past has been reinvented. At this point, armed with a common pool of knowledge, it's time to shift focus to the "Lead" side of the model. This is also a good place to break and let the players realign themselves for the next round.

Typically, there are a lot more opinions about *what went wrong* than there are about *what needs to be done differently.* The past is known and therefore much easier to recount. The future is another story—one that hasn't yet happened and is therefore difficult to talk about in specific terms. For those reasons, you may need to take a more active role in this half of the process.

Working the lead side also starts with the formation of a set of questions. However, this time each question is prefaced by *Now,* followed by *how?* and is keyed off one of the questions on the manage side. For example, take the questions from the sample sets above:

1. Team Performance or Productivity

- *Now* that we know who we are, *how* often should we get together?
- *Now* that we know why we're here, *how* do we proceed?
- *Now* that we've identified the problem, *how* do we solve it?
- *Now* that we know when it happened, *how* do we prevent it from happening again?

2. Customer Satisfaction or Service

- *Now* that we know who filed the complaint, *how* do we communicate with that customer?
- *Now* that we know why this customer is upset, *how* do we fix the problem?
- *Now* that we know what this customer wants, *how* do we provide it?
- *Now* that we know when this customer needs it, *how* do we get it there in time?

Like many new processes, this one takes some getting used to—especially the awkward use of *now* and *how*. I'm not sure why the *now-how* combination works, but it does help people to stay focused. The objective of this part of the exercise is to have the entire group gain a better *understanding* of the problem, a complete *awareness* of all aspects of the problem, and a sharper *perspective* on how the problem will be solved. This can be achieved in a short space of time and is far more practical than working your way through a meeting agenda.

As a rule of thumb, a functional organization, team, or individual should spend between 60 and 70 percent of its energy thinking ahead. Spending too much time on issues from the past is, in my view, dysfunctional. You can't change what has already happened, but you can influence how you respond next time.

Let's see how these models were applied to reverse the fortunes of an international manufacturing firm.

The company in this case preferred to locate its fabrication plants in rural areas, near small communities that were known to have a solid labor force with a strong work ethic. This strategy had served it well until recently. During the construction phase of the company's newest plant, the entire workforce of more than 500 employees, supervisors, and managers had received training in total quality management methods in addition to an extensive course in statistical process control at the local junior college.

The start-up went well. Equipment was installed properly, and check runs showed great promise. The first orders were cut to specifications and shipped on time without a hitch. For a while things were looking good. Then the customer complaint hot line started to ring. The majority of complaints fell into two categories: incorrect sizing and shorted orders.

At first, complaints trickled in, but they soon came in a steady flow. Try as people might, the source of the two basic complaints could not be pinpointed. Management called meetings and pushed quality control so hard that the workforce got uptight and threatened to form a union. The situation started to get out of hand.

The company president asked me to look at the new plant operation to see if I could help. I was fairly confident that the answers would be easier to find if I talked with the folks on the production line, so I arranged to visit the night shift upon my arrival.

The shift supervisor scheduled meetings with each of the production crews. Using the two models described above, each group worked its way through the process until the sizing problem was isolated and a resolution found. It turned out that two questions, *When does this happen?* and *Who is involved?* provided the key to the solution. It happened on runs with oddly shaped pieces, and it involved the machine operators.

Eventually, the sizing problem was traced to the local school board's decision to drop woodworking and metal shop from the junior high school curriculum several years back. Apparently these classes were the primary source for instruction in the use of a tape measure. Without that basic knowledge, the machine operators couldn't tell the difference between 1/16 and 5/8 inch on a tape measure.

To their credit, the machine operators would seek out someone with tape-reading skills to check the first piece of each run. But no further measurements were taken before the order was packed for shipping, so if the machines got out of alignment after the first piece, later pieces would be incorrect.

The answer to the *now, how* question led the company to the state office of education, where it received a grant to train the plant's entire workforce in basic arithmetic and calculation models.

The cause of the shortage problem was harder to find. The answer to *Where does it happen?* took us to the quality checkpoint at the end of the tempering process, where the fabricated pieces left the furnace. From there, the pieces were picked up by a robot arm and set on a conveyor belt to cool on their way to the final quality check.

When does it happen? pointed us to the checkpoint operator, who lifted each piece off the belt and laid it down on a metal frame with electronic sensors around the edges. If the piece didn't fit, a buzzer would sound, indicating rejection. Silence meant that the piece was ready to be wrapped for shipment to the customer. Now we knew the answer to *Why does it happen?* but we still didn't know how to fix the problem.

I wandered from line to line, waiting to hear a buzzer so I could see for myself what was causing the deviation. Sure enough, a buzzer went off nearby, and I quickly headed toward the sound.

The checkpoint operator saw me coming and nodded hello as he tossed several rejected pieces into the nearby dumpster. I stood beside him to see what he would do next; he did nothing but wait. The buzzer sounded sporadically for the next twenty minutes. As we talked between buzzes, he seemed very pleased with himself. Finally, I asked him if he was concerned about the high rate of rejection. "Nope," he said, cheerfully. "They know what they're doing. I just pass 'em when they fit and trash 'em when they don't." His face dropped when I asked him *how* "they" knew if he didn't tell them.

Later that night, all the checkpoint operators got together with the machine operators to answer the question, *Now that the checker's found a reject, how should he communicate this?* Confident that they had resolved the shortage problem, I left the crews to their tasks and returned to my hotel for some sleep.

During the next few months, I made several visits to the plant and was encouraged to find the process improvement models being applied throughout the facility. Production records were being set regularly, and employee turnover (a previous problem) was under control. Overall, the plant manager had every reason to be pleased with the results; the changes meant that his plant would reach the break-even point well ahead of projections.

Discussion Starter

If you are not sure that you want to use a real situation the first time you apply the manager/leader models, use this football story instead. It provides a great jumping-off point for a discussion on how easy it is for individual and organizational purposes to drift apart.

The Story

It's late in the first half, the score is 7–0, and the other team has just scored. After the kickoff, we have the ball on our own twenty-yard line with two minutes left until the half.

Our first-string quarterback was out with an injury. The second-string quarterback had been injured on the last possession, but he *might* be able to come back in the second half. The third-string quarterback, who has never before played in a real game, is about to take the field.

Nervous and excited, he listens as the coach gives him the following instructions:

"Listen carefully. It's important that you don't screw up and get us further behind. All I want you to do is kill the remaining two minutes so I can get into the locker room and come up with a new strategy for the second half. Here's what you're going to do: Call three running plays and then *punt*. No passes. No fancy stuff. Just hand the ball off three times and then kick it away. Got that?"

"Yes, sir!" says the third-stringer, and he runs out onto the field.

On the first play, the tailback breaks through for a long run to mid-field. (The crowd gets excited.) Next play, our hero hands the ball off to the fullback, who plows through for a thirty-yard gain. (The crowd goes wild!) On the third play, he hands off to the tailback again, who breaks free . . . only to be stopped just short of the goal line. (Now the fans are on their feet screaming.) On the fourth play, inches from a touchdown, the quarterback punts. (The crowd is stunned into silence.)

End of story.

When used in group discussions, this story can reveal a great deal about the group's acceptance and understanding of dysfunctional behavior. Responses vary, but typically the coach is blamed for not calling a time-out and sending in a new play. Comments on the quarterback are split. Some say that he should have gone for the touchdown, while others claim that he was just following directions. Rarely does anyone comment critically on the role of the other players.

The point of this exercise is to demonstrate how easily dysfunctional practices can impede the achievement of both individual and organizational purposes. As the exercise progresses, the participants are asked to consider the outcome from the perspective of the coach, the quarterback, and the team.

1. The *coach* was probably thinking how lucky he was to find a new star for his team. He was both surprised and delighted when the third-string quarterback did well, and saw no reason to call a time-out when things were going so well. What do you suppose went through his mind as he watched the quarterback punt the ball away?
2. The *quarterback* was *so* happy not to have screwed up. He'd gotten through his first real chance in a live game without a mistake, following his coach's directions to the letter.
3. Why didn't the *other players* say something when the quarterback called for a punt at the goal line? Could it be that they wanted him to fail? Maybe they wanted to teach the upstart a lesson. Maybe they didn't like they way he had come in and taken charge. Maybe they wanted to embarrass the coach and get back at him for something.

No matter how long the issues are discussed, there is rarely a consensus on whom to blame for the missed opportunity to score. There is however, little disagreement about the root cause of the problem: The team lacked the ability to shift focus when its purpose changed. Once you introduce the notion of dysfunction, the discussion often takes a very interesting and useful turn.

People start relating the story to what has happened to them and then begin to talk about why *their* team isn't working. As they gradually make the connection between individual and organizational purposes, the discussion centers on their workplace, and they begin to explore whatever dysfunctions might be keeping their organization from achieving its purpose.

14

Devising Strategy

Our propensity to create large organizations is stifling our ability to change direction quickly and without great upheaval. At a time when managers need to be fast, fluid, and flexible, we're holding on to an outmoded structural methodology that is dragging them down. Today, size and strength are no longer advantages. It is true that there is strength in numbers, but it is also true that the bigger they are, the harder they are to change.

How many celebrated companies have changed size, shape, or direction in the past decade? How many more are presented in a state of flux? In today's fast-paced, high-tech, consumer-driven marketplace, even companies with long histories of success are vulnerable to buyouts, mergers, or takeovers.

These current events give us a clue that we should be looking for alternative ways to respond to change. While we're at it, let's devise some new strategies that hasten the collapse of outmoded and unresponsive systems. We must break away from the one-style-fits-all mentality as rapidly as possible.

This point of view may be considered radical or unrealistic by dysfunctional managers. But if you can accept this notion, then you're ready to learn how to use a more strategically focused approach to change, one that will be less disruptive and easier for people in your position to manage. So, if it's that simple, why haven't we thought of it before now?

Our current organizational theories have been around since the Great Depression. Those terrifying years still influence the way we think today—probably more than we comprehend. When you stop and think about it, you'll realize that most senior executives in today's workforce received their education and training from people who lived through that horrific experience. As a result, we've spent the last fifty years strengthening our management structures so as to avoid another wide-scale collapse. So here we are three generations later, still building fortresslike institutions to ward off another depression.

We'll get into strategies later. First, let's analyze the structure of a typical organization to see how it works and how it affects you. That way, you'll understand how and why organizations become dysfunctional when their systems undergo change.

Under closer scrutiny, you can see that your organization is really made up of three subsystems, as shown in Figure 14-1. These subsystems each have core values, membership restrictions, and definite boundaries that can be strongly forti-

Figure 14-1. Overlapping subsystems model.

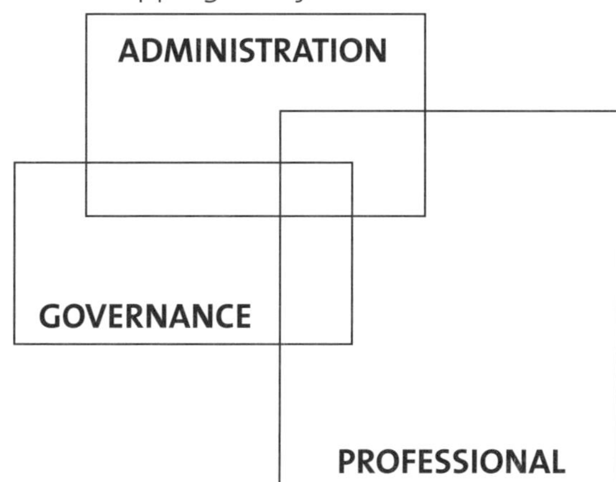

fied. Those who stray across borders, even when invited by their counterparts, may find themselves in a strange land indeed. The folks who inhabit each subsystem fiercely defend their territories, especially against outside influence.

If you've ever crossed one of these boundaries, you've probably encountered what Annette Simmons calls "the strategic noncompliance game, one of ten 'territorial behaviors' that run rampant in the workplace." Her book *Territorial Games: Understanding and Ending Turf Wars at Work* is based on in-depth research into "dysfunctional territoriality." Simmons provides a much deeper look into these games than we can give here.

The Subsystems

The size and influence of each subsystem depends to a great extent on the nature of the organization and its stage of development. For example, in a start-up company, the *professional* subsystem would be the largest at first. However, as the organization grows, the *administration* and *governance* subsystems will emerge and expand as the need for policies and procedures increases. At the peak of an organization's life cycle, the professional subsystem will still be the largest, but the administrative subsystem will have the most influence. As the company becomes rules-bound and slows down, the governance subsystem will enlarge and eventually dominate.

Before we look into how these subsystems interact with the larger organizational structure, let's take a deeper look at how they function separately.

Professional Subsystem

The professional subsystem is the most difficult to "see," but it is the easiest for most people to identify because it is the primary source of one's on-the-job persona. For example, when a coworker is introduced for the first time, the second thing that is said about this person, after the name, is what he or she does. This is frequently followed by where the person is located in the building. Later, you are more likely to recall what this new employee does or where he or she works than you are to recall the employee's name. Hence, your organizational identity is derived from the type of work you do or the company you keep.

The professional subsystem is made up of the various skill sets necessary to keep the organization running. Hospitals, for example, have doctors, nurses, technologists, and technicians plus a broad range of auxiliary services personnel, each with a specific set of skills. Some of these skills are complex and require extensive training, licensing, and continuous practice to stay current. Most of these folks belong to a group, association, society, or union that offers external rewards and recognition unrelated to their work assignments. Under adverse conditions, such as those created by change, these people's primary allegiance is often to their external connections rather than to the organization that pays them.

Administration Subsystem

The administration subsystem is the most visible. It can be seen on letterheads, stenciled on office doors, depicted on campus maps, and listed in phone directories. In addition, it is felt whenever the discussion turns to personnel resources, space utilization, or fiscal responsibility. The administration subsystem keeps track of the wages and salaries for all employee classifications. Traditionally, personnel or human resources functions, such as position descriptions, performance reviews, employment interviews, job vacancies, disciplinary actions, and promotion requirements, are all part of the administration subsystem.

Governance Subsystem

The governance subsystem is all about compliance with rules, regulations, and policies. It is typically visible in the form of boards, committees, commissions, and task forces where the law is officially interpreted and justice prevails. Sometimes the rules are changed without provocation or prior notification. Those who labor in the governance subsystem presume that everyone else is paying close attention to their deliberations and determinations. Rule changes and policy modifications flow from the governance subsystem in a steady stream. Few people are aware of the full impact this subsystem can have until they find they have violated a rule—after an IRS audit, for example. The power and influence of the governance subsystem can be rapidly expanded through connections to local, regional, and national governing bodies.

Subsystem Formation

This might be a good place to illustrate how the subsystems grow together naturally, then pull apart as the organization undergoes change. Start-ups are very good examples of how subsystems are formed, so let's step back and take a closer look at one.

This particular start-up was the brainchild of a group of medical doctors who wished to develop a new way of providing health care without the attendant high costs and personal stress associated with their solo practices. They acquired some land, put up a building, and opened for business. Along the way, a large health system agreed to refer patients to the new practice.

Things got off to a great start. They had no difficulty finding qualified staff. As the word got out about this new concept, job applications poured in. The newly elected board of directors hired a very capable medical-group administrator and a topflight operations manager. Working side by side, these two selected the rest of the employees. By the time they finished hiring, it's doubtful that a better staff could have been found anywhere else in the community.

The medical building was divided into an interconnecting series of expandable suites that would be filled one at a time as patient flow increased. In theory, this sounded great; in practice, it was unwieldy and difficult to implement. At first the physicians and staff had lots of time on their hands because of the low patient load. The doctors got used to seeing only one or two patients an hour and having the time to counsel and diagnose without being rushed. The slow pace gave the staff ample time to file records, greet patients, confirm appointments, check on tests, and take medical histories without the usual pressure associated with a busy office. From all indications, it was a happy, stress-free workplace.

But word quickly spread that the doctors at this new medical practice spent time caring for patients, and soon the influx of new patients overwhelmed the existing facilities. As patient flow increased, the staff in the main suite began to complain about increased workloads. In response, the manager pressured the administrator to open a second suite. But the board of directors withheld approval, saying instead that a predetermined level of income versus expenses had to be reached first. This level was not shared with the staff, however. All the while, additional patients kept coming and the pressure mounted to do more with less.

Some doctors were able to see more patients; others tried but just fell further behind. Before long the staff couldn't keep up and overtime was called for. The sudden increase in personnel costs prompted the board to open up a second suite. The board members believed that this would solve the problem. It didn't. It only set the stage for a repeat of the problems each time the patient load increased and another suite was opened.

A quick glance at Figure 14-2 gives you a sense of how the client subsystems looked. Clearly the professional subsystem was firmly entrenched and headed in its own direction. The administration subsystem existed mostly in the form of vendor contracts, supply inventories, bank statements, and billing records. Other than the occasional memo from the board of directors, there was very little evidence that the governance subsystem was present.

The first batch of medical assistants and clerical staff hired, all fifty-seven of them, reported to the operations manager. Following a

Figure 14-2. Individual subsystems model.

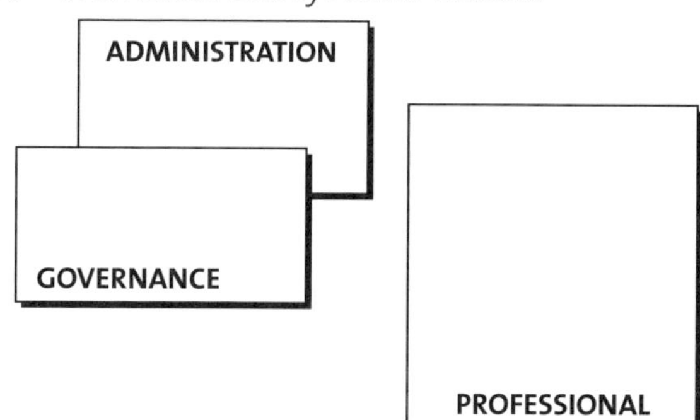

parallel track, the physicians addressed their concerns to the medical-group administrator personally. If the number of phone calls and the frequency of the overhead pages were any indication, lots of things were not working. Both the administrator and the operations manager complained that all they did most days was respond to pages and put out fires. Even though they felt they had hired good people, no one seemed capable of doing the job without calling for help. It didn't take long to find out why—a short visit to the employee lounge provided the answer.

It seems that the operations manager had told each employee at the hiring interview to "call me if you have any questions." So, when they got to their workstations and found no documentation, no job descriptions, no scheduling protocols, and nobody to train them, who do you think they contacted? This friendly gesture was interpreted as a directive.

It was amazing how fast the dysfunction had set in—only a few months after the opening. The huge disparity between the professional subsystem and the other two subsystems appeared to be the cause. Once this became known, the board of directors decided to strengthen the two weaker subsystems right away.

The entire workforce was brought together on a Saturday morning to assess the situation and do something to change it. The first assignment was to assess the current level of dysfunction. All were given copies of the dysfunctional behaviors checklist and asked to fill it out, but not to put their names on it. After the employees had completed the checklist, the papers were collected, and the items checked were tallied and then shared with the assembled group. The most frequently checked items were:

1. Corporate memory is lost or forgotten.
2. Requests for policy clarification are ignored.
3. People look for direction on how to act and react.
4. Friendship between professional colleagues is lacking.
5. Inconsistent application of procedures is not challenged.

The employees then knew what to address and where to start. They fished around for a theme that would define what they were about to do, one that would also engage the physician owners. Someone suggested that they treat the organization as they would a patient in need of urgent care. So a state of emergency was declared and prompt action was taken.

First, lead people were identified by their peers and given the authority by management to solve problems on the spot. Second, improvement teams were established to focus on the most poorly functioning processes. Third, an education committee was created to conduct a training needs assessment. More committees were formed to develop policies, procedures, and protocols. Finally, all employees were empowered to initiate changes that they felt would resolve patient problems, on condition that they documented the solution and forwarded it to management.

It took only a few weeks to overcome the dysfunction and get the place running smoothly.

Putting It Back Together

As you work your way through this section, keep in mind the following three assumptions:

1. *Change has become so rapid and unpredictable that more, not less, face-to-face discussion is needed in order to make intelligent strategic decisions.*
2. *Successful new strategies for increasing sales, producing quality products, improving customer services, reducing costs, and finding better ways of working together will be based increasingly on a manager's ability to influence all subsystems.*
3. *When people have a hand in developing change strategies, they are much more likely to carry them out. Getting people involved early will reduce months, even years, of potential resistance, misunderstanding, and low commitment later.*

Notice that in Figure 14-1, the three subsystems overlap to some degree. Organizational functionality is determined by the size of this common area; the larger the overlap, the more functional the organization. In other words, the more each subsystem's purpose is understood and supported, the more influence a manager in one subsystem can have in another. The objective, then, is for you to plug into all three subsystems, thereby enlarging your sphere of influence.

You've probably discovered by now that if it wasn't for change, we wouldn't be having this "conversation." But we can't ignore the fact that change creates turmoil and instability in most organizations. Just about the time you think all the subsystems have settled into a routine, one of them starts to change because of new personnel, different customer demands, redirectives from above, and the like. The resulting chain reaction pulls or drives the subsystems apart. As core beliefs become threatened, folks tend to pull in their outstretched arms and put up their defenses. To keep this from happening, you may have to reconnect with your counterparts in each subsystem.

At some point in the future, almost everything your team produces or provides will need to change. Applying the traditional organizationwide approach will only force you to increase performance demands or exercise more control. This means that in addition to managing day-to-day activities, you will also have to work with resistant people in pressure situations, smooth hurt feelings, and overcome the resulting dysfunction—a tough assignment even under favorable conditions.

The pressure to change can also frustrate top-level decision makers. In times like this, your boss may be reluctant to accept your recommendations without careful research and ample documentation. Typically, you can't afford the time to conduct feasibility studies or needs assessments. Whatever strategic functions exist in your company are usually focused on economic conditions and financial forecasts. Little attention is paid to your level, where the best ideas are more likely to originate.

A typical organization is not structured to encourage innovation and creativity from within. In fact, it usually burdens people like you with the thankless job of planning and development—two complex tasks that are neither fully understood nor appreciated.

Organizationwide changes are usually planned and professionally managed in order to minimize the chance of failure. Why not do the same for changes to the subsystems? That is one way of keeping the professional, administration, and governance subsystems in balance.

Your role, then, is to bring creative ideas to fruition by working with your colleagues to clarify the authority, responsibility, and relationship issues. Additionally, by pulling together, you can mutually perform the following functions, usually reserved for the higher-ups:

- Assess human resources productivity.
- Recognize, identify, and resolve intrasystem conflicts.
- Facilitate problem identification and resolution.
- Identify options and alternatives.
- Design implementation strategies.
- Determine training and development needs.
- Evaluate results and recommend changes.

Once the smoke has cleared and the purpose of a specific subsystem change is clearly understood and formally accepted, you and your colleagues will become the primary advocates for implementation. By the time the leaders from each subsystem have finished working with you in this venture, they will better understand the need for change and react to it in more positive ways.

The Depth of Change

The preceding section may have told you more than you ever wanted to know about subsystems. However, there's still a bit more for you to consider. Earlier, the subsystems were described as having core values, membership restrictions, and definite boundaries. It is these core values that determine the membership restrictions and define the boundaries of each subsystem. The strength of these core values coupled with a time frame will determine how long it should take for change to occur. Once both of these factors are considered, you can select an appropriate change strategy.

Managers struggle with organizational change for many reasons, some of which we've already covered. Figure 14-3 represents, in pictorial form, what I've found to be the least understood elements of change: time and depth. If the core values are deeply embedded, it will take either a long time or a lot of pressure to bring about change. On the other hand, if the core values are shallow or haven't taken root, change can happen quickly.

I've also discovered that for some people, the concept of core values is too abstract or remote unless they can apply it to their personal lives. Just in case that's where you are now, let me suggest that you take a moment to answer the following question:

Which would you find the easiest to do?

(a) *Change your clothes.*
(b) *Change your weight.*
(c) *Change your religion.*

The most obvious response is (a). But as you apply a time factor to each choice, you can see how the answer might be

Figure 14-3. Depth of change model.

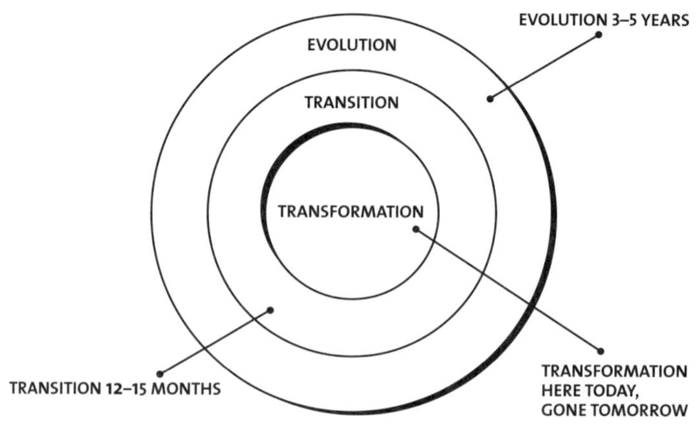

affected. For instance, let's say that you've already agreed to take part in your best friend's wedding, but you've just found out the cost of the required attire. You might wish now that you could change your mind instead of your clothes.

At first, you might think that response (b) would be a limited choice because a weight change is so difficult and time-consuming. But if your blood pressure is high and your doctor has told you to diet, you might be anxious to shed a few pounds. Or, how about the overweight boxer who's facing disqualification if the pounds don't come off before the next fight?

There's no doubt that to expect someone to change her or his religion is unthinkable. But people do become disillusioned with outmoded dogma and search for something more meaningful. Also, it's not uncommon for a person to change religions when he or she marries someone from another faith.

The key element in the above examples is *personal readiness.* In each case, the individual was motivated and ready to change. Introducing change before people are ready is like putting a dent in a polyester pillow. If you keep your head firmly in place, you'll make an impression. But it'll pop back out when you lift your head. Maybe that's the reason so many managers view change as a pain in the neck.

Just as individuals will change when they're ready, so will an organization change when its subsystems are ready. The trick is to get the subsystems and the people in them ready to change at the same time. Keep that thought in mind as you digest the following change strategies.

Evolution

This is the most widely known change strategy. It is more commonly called *long-range planning* because it implies that things will be different sometime in the future. Nowadays, a three- to five-year planning cycle seems to be a reasonable time frame. It allows plenty of time to absorb the potential effects of change before anything really happens. Folks are encouraged to consider how the change may affect them individually and collectively. Opportunities are provided for people to share their concerns with management. Periodically, the plans are modified and accommodations are made to ensure buy-in. Milestones are set. Goals are celebrated. The program is approved and the training schedule announced.

Transition

This is the most pragmatic change strategy; it is often referred to as *planned change.* It usually includes a major reorganization and involves just about everybody. The bottom line is brought clearly into focus as costs and profits are scrutinized. Attention is directed to projects with the highest rate of return. Marginal products and services are either dropped or put on hold. Research and development fights to stay afloat. Efficiency experts are hired to cut costs, eliminate waste, and get rid of the deadwood. Performance expectations and productivity targets are raised to match income forecasts. Frequently tied to the budget cycle, this change strategy has both a defined beginning and a desired completion date.

Transformation

This is the newest and most painful method in the strategic arsenal; it is better known as *downsizing* or *reengineering.* Management actions include drastic cutbacks, massive layoffs, and plant closures. Whole industries have been moved to new locations in pursuit of lower production costs. Often done to preserve what's left of an organization, it can be devastating to the unprepared. Usually kept under close wraps until the last minute, transformation catches people by surprise and sends shock waves throughout an industry. Transformation does have a positive side. Recovery is possible, and the benefits can be immediate if the transformation is designed as a reformation project. Like the phoenix rising from the ashes, a properly crafted transformation can resemble a miracle.

Strategic Solutions

The future vitality of your workplace will depend on its ability to change with minimum upheaval. By applying some of the methods described here, you can positively influence the way people in and around you react to change and, by doing so, help them succeed. That's not as far-fetched as it sounds; it can be and has been done. The following case study illustrates how a public service agency worked its way through a difficult and demanding transformational change.

The director of a regional social service agency had developed a national reputation for his innovative approach to automation at a time when computers were mostly used for record keeping. Congress had just approved a major overhaul of the welfare program, and included in the package were appropriations for state-sponsored pilot programs. While the other agency directors pondered the implications, Mr. K was first in line at the state capital. He came away with a fully funded computer system plus $9.5 million and a promise of more if the pilot program was in place by the end of the fiscal year—nine months away.

His first challenge was to break the news to the 2,000-plus employees. This was not an easy task. Most of the employees were aware that the welfare reform was coming and weren't looking forward to the change. They had no idea that their director had volunteered them as a national test site.

Mr. K broke the news to his department heads and program managers. Based on past experience, he anticipated some negative reactions. True to form, there were plenty. The major complaint was directed at Mr. K for not running this by them in advance. After all, this would be a huge undertaking, and they should have been consulted. He admitted that he had wanted to avoid the usual period of whining and complaining that had accompanied changes in the past. Tired of their dysfunction, he decided this time to make the change first, then deal with them later.

The room erupted with loud denials. Mr. K listened for a while and then posed this question to the assembly: *What would you have done if I had consulted you before going to the state?*

One by one, almost on cue, they put forth reason after reason for him not to take the risk with the whole nation watching. Amazingly, they did just what Mr. K said they would do—they tried to talk him out of it.

The venting and challenging went on awhile longer, but it faded to mumbling as it became evident that Mr. K wasn't backing off. Before anyone could speak, Mr. K stood up and headed for the door. He stopped short, pointed toward the group with a big grin, and bellowed, "You're the management team, do something!" Then he left. Startled, the group at first sat motionless. As they made eye contact with one another, smiles began to break out around the room. Soon, the room was filled with the energizing sounds of people ready to do something.

They spent the remainder of that meeting discussing the changes that must occur in the professional, administration, and governance subsystems, identifying the programs that would be most affected by the change, and assessing their personal readiness for this change. A few hours later, they sent for Mr. K and shared their plan with him. After a brief discussion and some procedural questions, he agreed to the concept and scheduled another meeting to work out the details.

Their scheme called for the formation of teams to represent each subsystem. From a list of 125 volunteers, they eventually picked 30 employees to undergo extensive training in change management, responsibility charting, problem solving, and a variety of assessment techniques specifically tailored for groups in transition. The employee group named itself the Be Team. Its motto, IF IT'S GOING TO BE, IT'S UP TO ME, was emblazoned on T-shirts, lapel buttons, and coffee mugs. Ghostbuster-like posters appeared in hallways and on bulletin boards urging people to call the Be Team if they had a problem.

Within a few months, the Be Team's influence was felt throughout the agency. The transition was by no means easy, and it wasn't completed as planned. But it did change the way the agency did business and got the agency where it needed to be. Mr. K contributed by persuading state officials to reset the deadline a time or two, which helped a lot. So did the national and state awards that followed the successful transition.

15

Reshaping Corporate Culture

The booming decade of the 1980s was a period of big deals and big profits. It seemed as if anyone who was willing to risk a few bucks was sure to prosper. Hopeful entrepreneurs flocked to investment seminars looking for the perfect franchise. "How-to" books filled the stores, while "get rich" gurus moved from city to city gathering converts. For a while, all you had to do to get a following was to "tell it like it is" (or at least *sound* as if you knew what you were doing).

If there was a downside, it was hard to spot. In many cases reality and truth were hidden by growth and expansion. A little-known business consultant became an overnight sensation by writing a book featuring the best-run companies in America at that time. Today, a large number of those companies have failed or are floundering. That's not as surprising as it might seem. This "go-go" period, as it was called, was the spawning ground for a lot of the workplace dysfunction we are facing today.

In the hard-driving 1980s, managers were taught that persistence paid off. The most dynamic of these creative risk takers were called "champions." They kept pushing their ideas again and again until, eventually, they worked. Many corporate watchers and management critics honestly believed that this particular entrepreneurial style got results, and to some extent they were right. But this "ready, fire, aim" philosophy also encouraged risk taking without due consideration of the fallout from failure.

Had we focused less on the success stories of that period and paid more attention to the failures, we might have learned some valuable lessons. A couple of well-known names come to mind; let's examine their downfall and see what we can discover. This time, put yourself in the story and see what lessons you might learn from the two cases that follow.

We'll start with the petroleum industry, which, thanks to the so-called energy crises, was riding the crest of an economic wave.

Gulf Oil and Chevron were particularly well positioned in the rush to find more domestic oil. Gulf seized the opportunity to invest in additional federal offshore leases. Chevron, although it was in a position to do the same, chose instead to take a different approach.

Rather than compete with Gulf in a bidding war for exploration rights, Chevron saved its cash and waited until Gulf had drilled more wells and located new deposits. Satisfied that Gulf's cash reserves were too lean to defend against a buyout, Chevron bought the majority of Gulf's stock and took control. Within a matter of months, Gulf dwindled in strength from several thousand employees to a mere handful of accountants and attorneys. Within a very short time, Gulf Oil Company ceased to exist at all.

The top brass at Chevron no doubt worked on their takeover scheme in secret. But bits and pieces must have leaked. After all, employees from Chevron and Gulf lived in the same neighborhoods, shopped at the same markets, and took their kids to the same schools. They knew each other's interests, problems, and concerns—all of which were grist for the rumor mill. Gulf's employees were bound to have heard rumblings of a takeover.

Let's suppose these rumblings had been brought to the attention of Gulf's decision makers. Would the information have been sufficient to alert management to the prospects of failure? Would senior managers have believed what their employees had heard and acted differently? Given the decision-making style of that era, it's doubtful. These managers would most likely have discounted any feedback that didn't support their views.

The oil industry didn't have exclusive claim to that top-down management style. If we look at the manufacturing sector, we'll find our second example: Singer.

Over the years, the Singer brand sewing machine had become a standard household item. By the mid 1980s, Singer had a well-known product and a solid hold on the market. Management, expecting an increase in product demand, introduced a technologically advanced sewing machine—one that automatically created blind hems and buttonholes and a host of various pattern stitches. Sales skyrocketed! The investment paid off handsomely—for a while. But the good times didn't last. By the end of the decade, most of what Singer had going for it had been lost.

Why had Singer failed, and what could be learned from it? It was a victim of a powerful, unforeseen combination of social, economic, and technologic changes. As women entered the labor force in significant numbers, they had neither the time nor the inclination to sew at home. Almost simultaneously, department stores introduced ready-to-wear garments made to fit all sizes, and dry cleaners offered tailoring services at affordable prices. It wasn't very long before domestic sewing was on the decline—along with Singer's sales figures.

The experiences of Gulf and Singer are alike in many respects. Both companies were victims of unforeseen developments. Gulf became one of the earliest casualties of the financial trend toward takeovers. Singer found itself on the losing side of a shifting market.

These cases serve as prime examples of the significant roles that risk and feedback play in determining success and failure. Gulf did not have a functional feedback mechanism in place to allow input from inside the organization to reach the top. And, even if Singer's salespeople had picked up on the downward buying trend, the information was not communicated to management. In both situations, management was entrenched in a dysfunctional environment in which the risks were high and the feedback low. Such a combination forces the decision makers to make assumptions about future events, since they have no way of tapping into information that could help them select better alternatives.

Lest you think that the above examples are exceptions or that they took place under unique circumstances, all you have to do is look around and you'll see the same things happening in today's computer world. The fortunes of Apple, Compaq, Gateway, Hewlett-Packard, IBM, Intel, Microsoft, and Packard Bell rise and fall almost daily. Some of these companies have learned from failure; others have not. Chances are that a failure will occur in your workplace some day, and when it does, you'll be one of the few who knows what to do.

Organizational Culture

When you are faced with a difficult decision, you try to minimize the risk of being wrong by gathering as much information as you can. Sometimes you are pressed for time, and therefore the amount of information you can access is limited. Making decisions with limited information is risky. When the degree of risk is very high and you can't get enough feedback to minimize it, you may put off making the decision until you have more information. On the other hand, if the decision is of little consequence and the risk is low, you may act quickly, because in the long run, you aren't that worried about failure. It's the combination of the degree of risk and the amount of feedback that determines your behavior.

The same holds true on a larger scale. The combination of the degree of risk and the amount of feedback also determines an organization's culture. These two factors are represented by the risk-feedback model (Figure 15-1), which identifies four possible organizational cultures. In this model, *risk* relates to decision making and *feedback* relates to information.

The functionality or dysfunctionality of an organization depends upon how the people in the organization react to failure, treat mistakes, serve customers, handle complaints, cre-

Figure 15-1. Risk-feedback model.

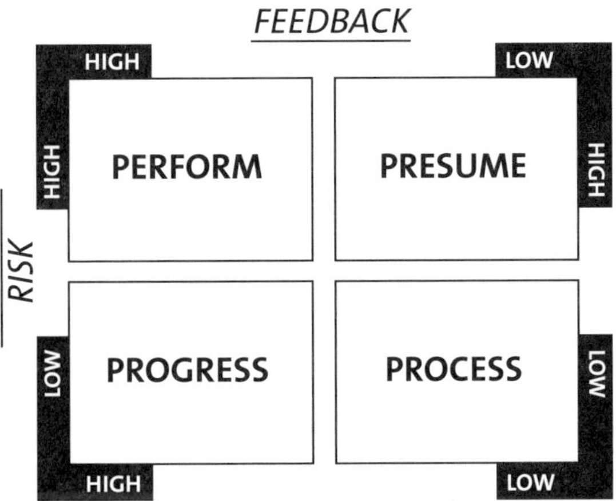

ate ideas, manage growth, and view success. As you review the description of each culture, make note of how that culture responds to failure and compare it to what goes on in your workplace.

Presume Culture (High Risk/Low Feedback)

- Crises are high priorities at most work levels.
- Employees move from one crisis to the next.
- People never know how well they are doing.
- Problems require a high-risk, bet-your-job type of decision making.
- Oportunities for making a difference are few.
- Chances of continued success are limited.
- Mistakes are not tolerated.
- The cost of failure is high.
- The norm is, avoid mistakes and be certain before you act.
- All possibilities of failure are double-checked before launch.
- New ideas are modest improvements on what worked before.
- Innovation means pirating something from another company.

Process Culture (Low Risk/Low Feedback)

- ⋆ There is little chance of failure, and the risk of being wrong is minimal.
- ⋆ Limited risk is matched by infrequent feedback.
- ⋆ Resistance to change is very strong.
- ⋆ Failure is viewed as an ending point or career stopper.
- ⋆ Once an idea fails, there is no interest in trying it again.
- ⋆ People keep track of failures.
- ⋆ New employees are told not to upset the status quo.
- ⋆ Customer service is slow and unresponsive.
- ⋆ Complaints are expected as part of the job.
- ⋆ Growth involves long periods of planning by many people.
- ⋆ Ideas and suggestions are carefully studied from every angle.
- ⋆ The organizational norm is, "Don't rock the boat."

Progress Culture (Low Risk/High Feedback)

- ⋆ Plans and creative concepts are developed for the future.
- ⋆ Employees strive for success and take chances.
- ⋆ There is time to develop and test new ideas.
- ⋆ The developmental focus is both near-term and long-term.
- ⋆ Failure creates opportunities for testing alternatives.
- ⋆ Information is available from easily accessible sources.
- ⋆ Failures don't keep people from rising up and trying it again.
- ⋆ People are fluid, moving often and changing positions and job duties.
- ⋆ Discussions jump from one idea to another without closure.
- ⋆ New projects are launched before the pilot is finished.
- ⋆ Customers respond to personal attention and frequent contact.
- ⋆ The more people put into the job, the more they get out of it.

Perform Culture (High Risk/High Feedback)

- The relationship between risk taking and feedback is balanced.
- Ample information to fully understand the risk is available.
- Risk stimulates creative thinking and builds confidence.
- The best decisions are made when the competition hesitates.
- Everyone spreads out to look for new information.
- People know how to network with unique and varying sources.
- Change is the natural way to sustain high performance.
- The goal is to keep ahead of the competition.
- Innovation means new ways to use existing resources.
- Failure is expected and is overlooked when it occurs.
- Customer response time is an important factor.
- New learning opportunities and creative processes are the norm.

Discussing Failure

Regardless of your organization's culture, your challenge is to make current decisions with the greatest possible knowledge concerning their potential for future success, to organize your team to carry out these decisions, and to measure the results. In some cultures, meeting this challenge is simply a matter of matching the degree of risk with the right amount of feedback. In a dysfunctional organization, unfortunately, you are often deprived of information (remember the hourglass model in Chapter 8). In that situation, the chances of failure increase each time you make an uninformed decision.

Failure, in and of itself, is not dysfunctional. It is the way each culture reacts to failure that determines its functionality. In some corporate cultures, failure is not tolerated. In others, it is an expected part of success. If you are like most managers, much of your willingness to risk depends upon your own view of failure. Successful managers understand the risk involved in any given situation and strive to overcome their fear of failure. That fear is constant in a dysfunctional organization. Confronting failure allows you to learn from it and overcome it so that it doesn't get in your way. It also helps you to mold your team in a positive way, even when the surrounding organization is dysfunctional.

Of the four corporate cultures, the *presume* culture is the most prone to dysfunction. This is a tense culture, fast-paced and crisis-driven. The people in it tend to be self-centered, close-minded, and mean-spirited. Succeeding in this culture is difficult, since both the risks and the chances of failure are high. Employees are typically closed to feedback. If they are open to it, they usually don't know where to look. The Gulf Oil and Singer stories cited previously are examples of what can happen to an organization that gets stuck in a presume culture. Gulf and Singer increased their risk without upgrading their feedback process. Eventually, the lack of usable information did them in.

A few years ago I was training a group of deputy sheriffs and experienced firsthand one of the dysfunctional aspects of a presume culture.

At 4:35 P.M. on a weekday afternoon, a natural disaster struck a nearby community. While this Sheriff's Office was the law enforcement agency closest geographically to the scene, that scene wasn't in its jurisdiction, and therefore these deputy sheriffs did not respond. When the State Emergency Services Disaster Reaction Team called at 5:15 P.M. requesting aid, nobody was there. Despite the disaster situation a few miles away, the deputy sheriffs had all gone home promptly at 5 o'clock—their regular quitting time. Fortunately, the sheriff was able to recall them quickly and send them rushing to the scene. Once there, they did an excellent job. In fact, in a nice bit of bureaucratic irony, the state eventually awarded them a citation for their outstanding service.

The *process* culture is also dysfunctional because the people in it are nonreactive. This is a slack culture, slow-moving and crisis-resistant. The people in this culture, while generally well intentioned, tend to be self-satisfied and close-minded.

They do not respond in a timely manner and therefore discourage creative solutions to pressing problems. Getting people to change the way they do things, even when such change is clearly justifiable, takes a major effort. Case in point: Consider the public's current dissatisfaction with government bureaucracies and educational institutions.

In both the process and presume cultures, employees change only when change is forced upon them. External demands for change put pressure on employees to make decisions sooner than they would like. They do so reluctantly and without asking for additional feedback. Thus they risk being wrong more often, which, in turn, increases their opportunity for failure. Given these circumstances, people naturally feel threatened by change. Rather than looking forward, they start wishing for the good old days and talking about how great things used to be.

Locating Dysfunction

Although by now you probably know what to do next, here is a strategy that has proven to be very effective. First, bring your team members together and share the risk-feedback model (Figure 15-1) with them. Ask them to discuss risk and feedback and to describe what they perceive as the way you react to failure. Add your view, and then lead a discussion on which culture best describes where they are now. If they pick a functional culture (perform or progress) and you agree with that assessment, lead a discussion on what it will take to stay there.

The progress culture is a good place to be. The level of dysfunction is usually low, and catching dysfunction at stages 1 or 2 is easier. You may not have any reason to reshape this culture. However, if you want to move your team along on a developmental track, the *perform* culture is the best place to go. To get there requires showing more initiative, which means that the risk of failure may increase. Before your team decides to act, have the team members check to see what feedback is available so that they can calculate the degree of risk they face. Once they have pooled their information and accepted the increased risk of failure, they are probably ready to move to the perform culture.

If your team believes it is in the perform culture, the trick is to stay there. Once your team is satisfied that where it is is where it needs to be, use the risk-feedback model as a framework to evaluate future risks. Reviewing the model periodically can help you and your team gain new insights while forging a sense of common values and purpose. As a result, you should be able to clarify the specific steps your team needs to take to ensure a successful future even if the organization as a whole becomes dysfunctional.

What if your team realizes it is in a dysfunctional culture (presume or process)? Then the discussion should focus on how to change that situation. Since the level of dysfunction is most likely to be at stage 3 (where ambiguities and inconsistencies are undiscussable), you must find a way to open up the flow of information. Even if you have to force-feed people, keep the information coming. Since most people in a dysfunctional culture are not used to asking questions to gain information, you may have to form the questions yourself. (And, at first, you may even have to provide the answers.) All is not lost: One positive thing about working in a presume or process culture is that if people don't have to act on the information, they'll cheerfully listen to whatever you have to say.

Strategic Components

As you begin to reshape your portion of the organization's culture, you may want to use a more structured process. Include the four strategic components outlined below when you formulate your plan. There are several ways to work your way through each of these components. One way is to do it on your own, or to consult with a small number of people you know to be truthful. The best way is to get your team away from work for a few hours and ask the team members to respond directly to each component. It doesn't really matter how you do it; the important thing is to get to it as soon as you can.

* *Environmental opportunities.* Identify those values and opinions that are related to what your team might do. Start by asking all participants to share the events, developments, and trends that they feel are currently affecting the team or forcing the need to change.

* *Interests and desires.* Determine the culture you are moving toward based on what your team wants to do. Assess each player's view of the changes that she or he feels the team needs to make. Each suggestion should be accompanied by a recommendation for what the team ought to do to minimize the risk of failure.

* *Organizational responsibility.* Clarify customer demands (both internal and external) and expectations for what your team should do. Determine how each player will work to ensure a successful outcome. Make a list of whose help and what resources will be needed. Decide how the required help and resources will be obtained.

* *Competence and resources.* Define the most successful course to take based on what your team can do. Set goals, establish time lines, determine priorities, and clarify the steps that need to be taken to ensure that the planned changes are fully understood and supported.

Afterword: Personal Choices

So where do you, personally, fit in to all this concern about dysfunction? How much risk you are willing to take will depend upon how you view failure. If you're like most managers, your success depends upon your personal efforts. In a dysfunctional setting, you may react to the many negative responses by withdrawing or limiting your efforts. It's normal also to misinterpret lack of support and appreciation as signs of failure. But this may not be true. Try to remember that by wanting to succeed in a dysfunctional workplace, you are upsetting the status quo and going against an established norm. As you continue to work with dysfunctional people, use the following principles to guide you:

- Think of risk as a means of measuring the value of your commitment. You risk failure whenever you commit yourself to a dream or vision. You risk losing support from others when you act on your own set of goals.
- Look on failure as part of the learning process. You will fail many times. Examine the cause and try to avoid similar mistakes in the future. Adopt a no-big-deal philosophy. When one thing doesn't work, don't give up—try something else.

* Have a strong belief in your worth and value. You may have faults (which others will quickly point out), but as a whole person, no one is better than you. Feel good about yourself and trust that what you do is right for you.
* Don't waste time with negative people. You will feel good about yourself when you are surrounded by people who hold you in high esteem. Do what you believe in and others will believe in you. Trust in others and they will support you.
* Do not compromise yourself and your values. Hold yourself up and treat yourself well. You deserve it!

Working with people in a dysfunctional culture is best done incrementally—a little bit more risk each time. Eventually people will understand that taking responsibility for their actions is not as risky as they thought. When you don't have the time to explore the consequences of failure with your team, go ahead and assume responsibility for the riskier decisions yourself. If your team members know that you are willing to confront failure, they are more likely to follow your lead in the future.

In dysfunctional settings, people don't know what success looks like, so you may have to "picture it" for them. Begin by describing what the situation looks like now. Make it clear that the current situation is unacceptable and that it must not continue as is. Help them understand why, and get them to accept the need for things to improve. Finally, state your goals and tell them what they can expect from you when the goals are reached.

As a manager, you are expected to produce results. Your biggest challenge as a manager in a dysfunctional environment is to produce results that are *appreciated.* In a dysfunctional organization, success is not an expectation, so don't expect much support in your search for excellence. If you do manage to make a difference, make sure people know that it was you who did it. But don't be surprised if few people notice or acknowledge your achievements.

If you are new to the organization, listen to the war stories to see which side usually wins. Find out who the "heroes and heroines" are, and learn how they achieved their fame. If what they did makes sense to you, set your goals higher and get to work.

Three factors are key to maintaining a sense of personal worth in a dysfunctional environment:

1. There must be opportunities for you to make a positive difference.
2. There must be opportunities for you to grow and develop.
3. There must be opportunities for you to do things that others cannot or will not do.

As long as all three factors are present, you may find satisfaction in your job even if your organization becomes (or remains) dysfunctional. However, if these opportunities diminish in value or cease to inspire you, it is likely that you can do no more. In that case, your next move would be to update your résumé and plan a graceful exit.

Influential Readings

Most of the material presented in this book has been derived from personal experience, acquired through years spent consulting and conducting training sessions in a variety of organizational settings. Additionally, I have been inspired by the work of several other professionals during that same period. Reading their books definitely helped shape some of my thinking and writing.

The following list highlights a number of these author/practitioners. I have found their concepts and ideas to be especially insightful—I hope you do, too.

Addesso, Patricia J. *Management Would be Easy . . . If It Weren't for the People.* New York: AMACOM, 1996. We work in organizations that are designed and run from a very mechanistic viewpoint and wonder why people are so much harder to manage than machines. The author translates the concepts of Psychology 101 in a way that makes practical sense to managers. The book is based on the premise that when organizations do not manage people well, it is often because their policies and procedures fly in the face of well-established psychological knowledge.

Astin, Helen S., and Carole Leland. *Women of Influence,*

Women of Vision: A Cross-Generational Study of Leaders and Social Change. San Francisco: Jossey-Bass, 1991. This book examines the achievements of women leaders who worked for educational and social justice in America from the 1960s through the 1980s. The authors show how women leaders of the last few decades have redefined the very language we use to speak of leadership—sharing the vision, personal commitment, risk taking, and empowerment—and have influenced the way we *work* for social and organizational change.

Borysenko, Joan. *Guilt Is the Teacher, Love Is the Lesson.* New York: Warner Books, 1990. In this life-affirming book, the author frees the child within us from shame in all its guises: from the fear of success to the fear of failure; from alcoholism and workaholism to pessimism, bitterness, and hostility. Filled with exercises and information, this book provides a guide to help us seek out and understand the reasons for failed relationships, disappointing careers, and even some illnesses.

Farson, Richard. *Management of the Absurd: Paradoxes in Leadership.* New York: Simon & Schuster, 1996. Farson questions the current management fads and leadership techniques. He argues that there are too many meetings and that too much information is being passed around in the name of good communication. The author maintains that efforts to democratize the workplace have done little to increase worker participation and that hierarchy is still firmly in place in most companies.

Grof, Christina. *The Thirst for Wholeness: Attachment, Addiction, and the Spiritual Path.* New York: HarperCollins, 1993. The author addresses the question of how to survive in a nonsupportive or hostile world. Through personal anecdotes and the insights gained from nearly two decades of leading-edge work, Grof delineates the crucial issues underlying the addictive process and the spiritual quest.

Harrington-Mackin, Deborah. *The Team Building Tool Kit: Tips, Tactics, and Rules for Effective Workplace Teams.* New York: AMACOM, 1994. How do you turn a diverse group of employees into an effective team? This problem-solving reference spells out guidelines and gives easy-to-grasp tips and tactics for managing the human factors and nitty-gritty details that can hamper teamwork. The author explains how to define roles and responsibilities, select team members, encourage positive behavior, facilitate participation at team meetings, maintain control, evaluate and reward teams, and determine training needs.

Helgesen, Sally. *The Female Advantage: Women's Ways of Leadership.* New York: Doubleday/Currency, 1990. The author's findings reveal innovative organizational structures and strategies that will benefit everyone. She shows, for example, how the workplaces run by women tend to be "webs of inclusion"—communities in which sharing information is key, and the rules of the hierarchy come undone at unexpected points of contact. While male leaders tend to champion the value if *vision,* women leaders concentrate on developing a *voice.*

Kaminer, Wendy. *I'm Dysfunctional, You're Dysfunctional: The Recovery Movement and Other Self-help Fashions.* Reading, Mass.: Addison-Wesley, 1992. The author indicts the proliferation of twelve-step groups, best-selling recovery books, and quick-fix techniques and explores the effects of this billion-dollar industry on our culture. Kaminer argues that in the name of *individualism,* these movements market authority, encouraging mass conformity. Controversial, original, and brilliantly reasoned, this book will change the way we think about self-help.

Keen, Sam. *Fire in the Belly: On Being a Man.* New York: Bantam Books, 1991. Noted author and respected philosopher Sam Keen daringly confronts outdated rites of passage that impoverish, injure, and alienate men. The author reevaluates men and sex, men and war, and men and work, and then provides new models to help men move from brokenness to wholeness in every aspect of their lives. The story of injury and promise that Keen tells is relevant to both sexes.

Leonard, George. *Mastery: The Keys to Success and Long-Term Fulfillment.* New York: Penguin Books, 1992. Best-selling author George Leonard explains how the process of mastery will enable you to vault over the pitfalls of the quick fix to attain a higher level of excellence and a deeper sense of satisfaction. Whether you're seeking to improve your sport, your career, or your intimate relationships, you can take advantage of the five keys to mastery described in this book.

Mann, Rebecca B. *Behavior Mismatch: How to Manage "Problem" Employees Whose Actions Don't Match Your Expectations.* New York: AMACOM, 1993. This book shows how to understand and resolve the maddening differences that typically arise between managers and staff. But "bad" employees or poor supervisory skills are frequently not the true cause of conflict. The core problem lies in a mismatch of expectation and behavior. The author spells out practical techniques for handling just about every mismatch you're likely to face.

Morrison, Ann M. *The New Leaders: Guidelines on Leadership Diversity in America.* San Francisco: Jossey-Bass, 1992. This is the first book to reveal the country's "best practices" for promoting white women and people of color and to offer a step-by-step action plan for creating diversity strategies that achieve measurable results. Morrison presents specific recruitment, development, and accountability tools that foster diversity and help organizations—regardless of size, sector, location, or industry—to compete effectively for the best management employees available.

Noer, David M. *Healing the Wounds: Overcoming the Trauma of Layoffs and Revitalizing Downsized Organizations.* San Francisco: Jossey-Bass, 1995. This pioneering book tackles what may be the most complex organizational issue since the industrial revolution: the fundamental and irrevocable shift in the psychological contract between employee and organization. Based on case studies and original research, this book provides clear guidelines for revitalizing a downsized organization. It also offers layoff survivors specific coping mechanisms so that they can understand and transcend the toxic effects of the experience.

Pool, Robert. *Beyond Engineering: How Society Shapes Technology.* New York: Oxford University Press, 1997. Pool demonstrates how seemingly minor decisions made early in the process of technological development can have profound consequences further down the road. The author explains how the increasing complexity of technology creates uncertainty, making it impossible to predict how well a technology will perform. This is an illuminating account of how technology and the modern world shape each other.

Schaef, Anne Wilson, and Diane Fassel. *The Addictive Organization: Why We Overwork, Cover Up, Pick Up the Pieces, Please the Boss and Perpetuate Sick Organizations.* New York: Harper & Row, 1988. A decade later, this book is still a relevant read. The authors reveal how the addictive system operates, how to recognize it, and how to begin the recovery process. This book describes how managers, workers, and members exhibit the classic symptoms of addiction: denying and avoiding the problem, assuming that there is no other way to act, and manipulating events to maintain the status quo. The richness of this work will open many doors to those trying to understand why change, excellence, innovation, imagination, and creativity are hampered in today's organizations.

Schmidt, Warren H. and Jerome P. Finnigan. *TQ Manager: A Practical Guide for Managing in a Total Quality Organization.* San Francisco: Jossey-Bass, 1993. The authors provide a concise guide for managers who are striving to develop the critical skills required for success after a quality initiative has been implemented in their organization. It helps managers deepen their understanding of TQM, identify the specific areas where improvement is needed, and create a plan of action for building skills.

Simmons, Annette. *Territorial Games: Understanding and Ending Turf Wars at Work.* New York: AMACOM, 1998. Territorial games are the unfortunate reality of the workplace, says the author of this provocative and practical book. But the good news is that these games are more like bad habits than like entrenched, compulsive behaviors. This book supplies positive strategies for combating workplace turf wars. And it shows you how to defuse all those acts of gamesmanship that detract from your own—and your organization's—success.

Tannen, Deborah. *You Just Don't Understand: Women and Men in Conversation.* New York: Ballantine Books, 1991. The author has written a refreshing and readable account of the complexities of communication between men and women. Aside from the vivid examples and lively prose, what makes this book particularly engaging is that the author makes linguistics interesting and usable. This book will help many put their problems of communication with the opposite sex in a manageable perspective.

Wheatley, Margaret J. *Leadership and the New Science: Learning About Organization from an Orderly Universe.* San Francisco: Berrett-Koehler, 1994. Wheatley shows how revolutionary discoveries in quantum physics, chaos theory, and biology (the new science) provide equally powerful insights for transforming how we organize work, people, and life. It sheds new light on issues that trouble people in organizations most: order and change, autonomy and control, structure and flexibility, planning and innovation. This is an easy-to-read, single-source summary of new science discoveries that will forever change your understanding of leadership, organizations, and life.

Wolin, Steven, and Sybil Wolin. *The Resilient Self: How Survivors of Troubled Families Rise Above Adversity.* New York: Random House, 1993. Writing with great warmth and understanding, the Wolins identify for the first time the clusters of strengths or resiliencies that typically emerge as survivors battle adversity. Around these resiliencies, they affirm the survivor's capacity for self-repair. This book will open readers' eyes to their own resilience and demonstrate how to replace a victim's mind-set with survivor's pride—the deep self-respect that comes with knowing that you've been tested and you've prevailed.

Bibliography

Aamodt, Michael G., and Wilson W. Kimbrough. "Effect of Group Heterogeneity on Quality of Task Solutions." *Psychological Reports* 50 (1982), 171–174.

Bennis, Warren, and Burt Nanus. *Leaders: Strategies for Taking Charge.* New York: Harper & Row, 1985.

Bridges, William. *Managing Transitions: Making the Most of Change.* Reading, Mass.: Addison-Wesley, 1991.

Bridges, William. *Surviving Corporate Transition: Rational Management in a World of Mergers, Layoffs, Start-ups, Takeovers, Divestitures, Deregulation, and New Technologies.* New York: Doubleday, 1988.

Brubaker, L., J. Loxley, and J. Voorhees. *Management Skills Assessment Program: Assessor Training Guide.* Berkeley: University of California, 1982.

Fournies, Ferdinand F. *Why Employees Don't Do What They're Supposed To Do and What to Do About It.* Blue Ridge Summit, Pa.: Liberty Hall Press, 1988.

Galbraith, Jay R. *Designing Complex Organizations.* Reading, Mass.: Addison-Wesley, 1973.

Hart, Lois B. *Learning From Conflict: A Handbook for Trainers.* Reading, Mass.: Human Resource Development Press, 1991.

Lawler, Edward. *Creating High Performance Organizations: Practices and Results of Employee Involvement and Total Quality Management in Fortune 1000 Companies.* San Francisco: Jossey-Bass, 1995.

Marston, William Moulton. *The Emotions of Normal People.* Minneapolis: Persona Press, 1979.

Noer, David M. *Healing the Wounds: Overcoming the Trauma of Layoffs and Revitalizing Downsized Organizations.* San Francisco: Jossey-Bass, 1995.

Schaef, Anne Wilson, and Diane Fassel. *The Addictive Organization: Why We Overwork, Cover Up, Pick Up the Pieces, Please the Boss and Perpetuate Sick Organizations.* New York: Harper & Row, 1988.

Shaw, Marvin E. *Group Dynamics: The Psychology of Small Group Behavior.* New York: McGraw-Hill, 1971.

Simmons, Annette. *Territorial Games: Understanding and Ending Turf Wars at Work.* New York: AMACOM, 1998.

Index